COLLINS GEM

BIRD
WATCHING
PHOTOGUIDE

Text by Rob Hume

Pho
Da

HarperCollins*Publishers*

HarperCollins*Publishers*
PO Box, Glasgow G4 0NB
First published 1995

Reprint 9 8 7 6 5 4 3 2 1 0

The copyright in the photographs belongs to the following photographers from the Frank Lane Picture Agency: L. Batten 114, 152, 204; R. Bird 72; H. D. Brandl 99, 127, 206; W. Broadhurst 71; M. Callan 119, 161, 218; A. Christiansen 81; H. Clark 146; P. Dean 108; G. Hakansson 173; A. R. Hamblin 7*l*, 12, 20, 53, 54, 70*t*, 84, 121, 131, 136, 139, 142, 149, 151, 158, 165, 170, 183, 217, 226; H. Hautala 143; J. Hawkins 51, 58, 61, 80, 106, 115, 145, 156, 159, 164; P. Heard 74; B. Henry 160; M. Holling 212; D. Hosking 18, 24, 36, 38, 39, 41, 60, 97, 132, 167, 179, 185, 191*b*, 215; E & D Hosking 4, 8, 10, 22, 32, 34, 45, 47, 68, 73, 75, 77, 90, 93, 100, 101, 104, 112, 118, 137, 155, 175, 177, 178, 180, 191*t*, 192, 195, 197, 201, 202, 207, 223; D. Jones 150; D. Kinzler 85; M. Nimmo 122; P. Perry 194; F. Polking 23, 221; P. Reynolds 91, 162, 203; D. A. Robinson 11*b*, 113, 141; Silvestris 105; M. J. Thomas 94, 109, 138, 154; R. Thompson 50, 186; R. Tidman 21, 40, 57, 89, 103, 111, 140, 144, 157, 168, 169, 174, 176, 182, 184, 187, 193, 213, 227; B. S. Turner 135; M. Walker 123; J. Watkins 65, 110; A. Wharton 63; R. Wilmshurst 5, 6, 7*r*, 9, 11*t*, 13, 15, 19, 31, 52, 55, 56, 59, 62, 64, 67, 70*b*, 92, 95, 96, 98, 107, 117, 124, 125, 126, 128, 130, 133, 147, 148, 163, 172, 189, 199, 211, 219; D. P. Wilson 166; W. Wisniewski 134, 200, 214; M. B. Withers 120, 129, 153

ISBN 0 00470756 7

Typeset by TJ Graphics

Printed in Italy by Amadeus S.p.A.

CONTENTS

INTRODUCTION

WHAT IS A BIRD?

Of all living things, birds are the most lively, colourful, easy to watch and accessible. There are birds from pole to pole; near the tops of the highest mountains; from the middle of the oceans to the hottest deserts. But what distinguishes these successful creatures from other forms of life?

● Flight: but some do not fly, while insects and even some kinds of mammals do.
● Eggs: but insects and reptiles also lay eggs.
● Feathers: this is the attribute that makes birds unique. Some feathers are hair-like plumes, others are so short and stiff that they are scaly. But nothing else has feathers. Feathers covering most of the body, wings – which are specialised fore-limbs – and a bill create a basic pattern; but within that theme is immense variety.

Developed from dinosaurs?

Birds evolved from warm-blooded, fast-moving dinosaurs. They share features with reptiles, such as scaly feet, but they are warm-blooded,

A house sparrow is familiar but is a good example to illustrate the bony sheath on a bird's beak; they also have hard, scaly feet with sharp claws

4

relying on their internal metabolism to maintain a constant body temperature rather than direct warmth from the sun, as in cold-blooded reptiles and insects.

Evolution has worked for many millions of years to diversify birds. Where there is food, there will almost always be a bird to exploit it, with adaptations that allow it to survive. Some birds have an extremely specialised way of life. The oilbird of South America lives in caves, finding its way in the dark by using echoes, like a bat, and feeding solely on certain fruits. Other more familiar examples

The dipper is a specialist bird: it feeds only in and around water and cannot survive elsewhere

include the treecreeper, which lives its entire life on the bark of trees and the dipper, which is never away from clean, running water. Other birds are more adaptable. House sparrows can live in cool, damp north-west Europe, and in desert oases. Herring gulls feed on scraps on top of Snowdon, on fish offal around ports and shellfish on the beach. Kestrels are at home in the city of London, the New Forest, on Scottish sea cliffs and on blisteringly hot Egyptian pyramids.

WHAT IS A SPECIES?

A species is a kind of animal or plant that can interbreed and produce healthy, fertile young, but which cannot breed with any other species. A dog is a species: Labradors, spaniels and red setters are varieties, or breeds, of dog. All can interbreed to produce healthy puppies. Robins, blue tits, blackbirds and song thrushes are not varieties or breeds. All are species. They cannot interbreed: otherwise the distinctions between them would become blurred and they would lose their individuality as species. As they are really distinct species we are able to recognise them – together with 9,000 species worldwide.

Species are remarkably constant. Every robin looks like every other robin. Every blue tit has the same pattern and colour, down to minute detail, as every other blue tit.

Field guides to identification give the most detailed descriptions to tell species apart. Sometimes it may be the pattern on a feather, the colour of the eye, or even the length of one feather next to another. These details are the same for every bird of the same species.

Robins interbreed: they will not mate with other birds such as house sparrows or song thrushes. The robin is a separate species

It is astonishing how reliable such differences are, although we tend to take them for granted.

Variations

There are variations, of course. Male blackbirds are black; females dark brown; young ones reddish-brown. These are differences of age and sex. Others are due to the time of year. A starling is glossy black with green and purple reflections in summer. In winter it has creamy-white spots. The mallard in breeding plumage has a glossy green head, white collar and grey body. In summer it becomes blotchy brown.

While species are generally remarkably constant, there are individual variations and also differences according to age or sex: here is a female (brown) and a male (black) blackbird

CHANGING COLOURS

Changes happen in two ways. The starling has cream tips to fresh feathers. By spring these wear away and the glossy colours that have been hidden beneath all winter are fully exposed. The mallard changes its bright feathers for dull ones in the process known as moult.

As well as wear and moult, birds become duller and less neat and tidy when their feathers are old and worn out. A winter robin is fresh and vivid; by mid summer it is pale and faded, lacking the brightness of its fresh feathers.

There are these individual variations, but the really remarkable thing is not the variation but the constancy in the outward appearance of birds. A robin is a robin, anywhere, any time.

The value of feathers

Nearly all birds change their feathers once a year. Some very large ones, like big eagles, take longer. Others change some feathers more often.

This herring gull is moulting: as new, paler, greyer wing feathers and whiter body feathers grow, it loses its mottled brown juvenile pattern

Feathers keep a bird warm, yet also protect it from hot sun. They give the bird its colours: bright and obvious, to show off to other birds, or dull patterns that help them hide away. Most importantly, they allow the bird to fly.

Worn or damaged feathers reduce their insulation and slow the bird down in flight. It must keep its plumage in top condition. It preens, drawing feathers through its bill to 'zip' them together. It scratches, to make the feathers lie neatly in the right order. It smears oil from its preen gland over feathers to keep them supple.

Some birds bathe in water and dust. They sunbathe, which probably helps feather care, or cover themselves with live ants, using the ants' formic acid to kill parasites.

This starling is preening to keep its plumage in good condition

MOULT: A STRICT ROUTINE

Each species follows its own order and timing for its moult, often different from similar species. The large wing feathers and tail feathers give a clue to the state of moult. These are replaced, one or two at a time, in a regular order. The first to be dropped signifies the onset of moult while, by the time the last is replaced, all the other feathers will have been replaced.

A baby blackbird leaves the nest in 'juvenile' plumage. By autumn it has moulted its head and body feathers into 'first winter' plumage, but the same juvenile wing and tail give away its age. Only in later moults does it begin to look like an adult.

The juvenile blackbird is brighter than a female and shows paler spotting on the upperparts

A chaffinch moults in the autumn into a fresh plumage. The feathers have brown tips, so chaffinches in winter look quite dull. When these all crumble away in spring, the male becomes much brighter, cleaner blue on the head, red-brown on the back and pink underneath.

Birds can also change the way they look by their posture. Chaffinches have big white flashes on their wings and tails, which momentarily distract a predator as they fly to escape. The white mostly disappears when the chaffinch lands, with its wings folded and tail closed, but it can droop the wings to show off the white to other chaffinches in special displays. You will see males with striking white patches displaying to females, but when they feed and want to be inconspicuous, the white is covered up.

◀ The male chaffinch in winter has buff-brown feather tips which give a dull overall appearance

▶ In summer the dull tips crumble away to reveal brighter, cleaner blue-grey and pink underneath

COLOURS AND COMMUNICATION

Adult robins have orange-red breasts. The one pictured below is a juvenile, just out of the nest. It is brown and spotted, so that it is hard to see under the shade of a hedge or on the edge of a ploughed field.

Robins threaten other robins, and defend their territories, by using the red breast. In the autumn the young robin needs to find a territory of its own. With its first moult, it gets its red feathers.

A juvenile robin must avoid attack from adult robins; its mottled brown breast lacks the red, which stimulates aggression

Here we see another reason why it was brown before. The adult robins, seeing the red, now treat their offspring as rivals: the red stimulates them to drive the young away. While they still need to be fed by their parents, young robins must lack red, so as not to trigger off the wrong response from the adults.

The great crested grebe uses its black crest and bright chestnut facial ruff in special spring courtship displays. During the nesting season the expanded ruff makes grebes look big and aggressive in territorial fights.

These adornments are of no use in winter: they simply get in the way. Grebes gather in flocks in winter and need to live side by side without constant bickering: the ruffs trigger off aggression. For winter, grebes moult, losing the colourful ruffs and gaining a blank white face instead.

Baby grebes need to be fed for several weeks and must be instantly recognised by their parents. They must not look like rival adults, so they have a dull brown plumage with black and white striped heads, a pattern that stimulates their parents to feed them.

Great crested grebes signal to each other and synchronise their breeding condition by using ear tufts and ruffs in their stylised displays

AVOIDING AGGRESSION: black-headed gulls

Gulls are intensely social creatures. They use their appearance, especially the colours of the bills, eyes and heads, to communicate in the breeding season. Outside the breeding season, they need to get along more easily without continual fighting: so the signals that were so vital in spring are lost. It is the regular sequence of moults that allows this change to take place.

Brown for safety

A juvenile black-headed gull has to avoid being mistaken for an intruding adult at the nest by its parent. Any adult gull would be attacked and driven off. A flightless juvenile would have no chance to escape and could be killed.

The juvenile is mostly brown, showing its silvery-white wing pattern only when it flies. The brown is good camouflage so that predators cannot see it so easily. It also makes it instantly recognisable by its parents when they return from a fishing trip.

Black-headed gulls lose their hoods in winter

Almost as soon as it flies from the nest, the juvenile begins to moult its head and body feathers, losing much of the brown. It changes from 'juvenile' to 'first winter' plumage.

The following spring, it moults its head and body feathers again: into 'first summer' plumage. The wing and tail feathers are still the same ones that it grew in the nest.

◄ A juvenile black-headed gull has brown markings for camouflage

▶ Adult black-headed gulls in summer use their brown hoods for signalling and courtship displays

Adult summer

Adult winter

Different plumages of the black-headed gull

In the late summer, when the black-headed gull is a
little over a year old, it moults once more. This time
all the feathers are replaced: it develops 'second
winter' plumage, which is the same as the adult's.
Larger species of gulls take three or four years to reach
adulthood.

The wing and tail feathers are new, ready to last
another full year. The head is white except for a black
spot. The bill and legs are scarlet. These are typical
colours of winter plumage black-headed gulls.

By spring, the gull will be ready to find a mate and
claim a nesting territory. It moults again, into summer
plumage, gaining an immaculate dark brown hood
except for conspicuous white 'eyelids'. The bill and
legs also change, to a deep plum-red. This is the

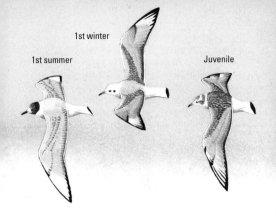

1st winter

1st summer

Juvenile

black-headed gull at its best, in superb summer plumage and ready to do battle.

The dark hood is the signal for dominance and aggression as well as a means of communicating to its mate. It lasts for the breeding season but, as soon as the need for such dominance is over, the next moult begins. The forehead turns white so that the threatening dark mask is quickly lost. Then the moult proceeds: another complete autumn moult, with the whole plumage replaced. The wings and tail often look ragged, with big gaps, during this autumn moult.

For the rest of its life the gull will continue this sequence, the head and body feathers being replaced every spring; the whole plumage, including tail and wings, every autumn.

SIZE AND SHAPE

Bird sizes and shapes are matched to the way they live. Small, slender warblers slip easily through leaves while they look for tiny insects and caterpillars. Long-legged herons wade in water, ready to strike out with their sharp, dagger-like bills to catch fish. They have long necks with a 'kink' in the middle, to give them a long reach and lightning jab.

Shaped by their food

Many birds are equally well adapted to special feeding methods. These may be very obvious, like an avocet's upcurved bill, which lets it lean forward and slide the bill from side to side through water and wet mud until it feels its food: tiny shrimps. Others may not be so visible, such as the green woodpecker's tongue, which is so long that it curls back around the skull. When it is fully extended it can probe the burrows inside anthills and catch ants on its sticky, barbed tip.

Usually the shape of a bird and its bill give good clues to its way of life. Many small birds have thin bills, designed for catching insects. Others, such as

The avocet's bill is specially shaped for catching small food in saline water and very wet mud

the house sparrow and greenfinch, have heavy, triangular bills, made for crunching seeds. Wading birds may have short bills (like the ringed plover) for picking food from the top of sand or mud; medium-length bills for picking up tiny crabs or shellfish; strong bills, like the oyster-catcher's, for breaking into mussels, or long, sensitive bills, like the curlew's and snipe's, for probing deep into wet mud and finding worms by touch.

Because they are so finely adapted, most birds have to have their particular habitat to survive: to protect them, the habitat has to be conserved. Snipe cannot live on dry ground: herons cannot survive without water.

Greenfinches peel the husk from seeds and crack the kernels with their strong, sharp-edged beaks

19

TIED TO A WAY OF LIFE

Ducks, geese and swans give good examples of birds dependent on special habitats. Mute swans need water deep enough for them to swim but no deeper than the length of their head and neck. They need to drag waterweed from the bottom and can reach deeper than ducks when they lean forward ('upend') and reach down with their long necks.

Grazers and dabblers

Geese graze on more open ground but need open water to be safe from foxes at night. Some species feed on arable fields or pastures. Others, like the brent goose, prefer mudflats and salt marsh.

Wigeon feed on damp grassland and marshes as well as in shallow water

Brent geese prefer eel-grass and green algae on coastal mudflats but also feed in fields

Wigeon feed in flocks on short grass, in wet meadows or on salt marshes. They crop the sweetest grass with their short bills. Mallards dabble in the shallows, finding seeds and snails at the water's edge, as well as feeding in fields on fallen grain.

Diving ducks feed under water. Tufted ducks dive by day to take animal matter; pochards feed more at night and eat more plants. Goosanders have hooked bills with serrations which they use to grasp slippery fish.

Predators

Birds of prey are adapted to special lifestyles, too. Hawks are short-winged and long-tailed for manoeuvrability in tight spaces: they are woodland bird-catchers. Buzzards are broad-winged, able to soar in the air while searching for small rabbits and voles.

Kestrels look for food from a stable position as they hover in midair

A specialised fish-eater, the osprey catches its prey in its feet

The kestrel hovers in one spot, searching for voles in rough grass, or watches from a perch. The peregrine, also a falcon, is a bird-hunter and specialises in fast, steep dives high in the air. Merlins catch small birds by chasing them until they tire.

Eagles soar at great heights, looking for prey and carrion. They eat dead sheep and deer but kill hares, using their powerful feet to squeeze and stab their prey. Ospreys specialise in fishing, diving headlong but hitting the water feet-first. They have very long claws and spiny feet to help grasp fish.

Steeplejacks

Woodpeckers have special features that fit them well for their way of life. Strong toes with curved claws give a secure grip on tree trunks. Two toes face forwards, two back (one of which can be splayed sideways) to get the best hold. Stiff tails act as props. Their bills are pointed and strong, to chip into bark for hidden beetle larvae or chisel away wood when making nest holes.

Slipping and sliding

Warblers show more subtle adaptations. Most are slim and sleek, to slip through close vegetation: reeds, leaves, grasses, thickets of nettles. The 'leaf warblers' are delicate, mostly green, yellow and white; the 'scrub

warblers' of lower levels are stouter and browner, with stronger legs and bills. The 'reed warblers' are dull, soft brown, with strong feet to let them grip vertical stems instead of perching across horizontal ones.

Reed warblers live in a strange world of dense, upright stems

Seed-splitters

Finches are seed-eaters with triangular bills, but show variety within this theme. Bullfinches' rounded bills squeeze buds and peel the skin from soft fruits. Siskins' and goldfinches' longer, pointed bills reach into the cones of alders and pines and inside the spiny depths of teasel and thistle heads. Greenfinches crack large seeds and nibble away the husks of heavy grains.

There are many more adaptations to particular ways of life. Some finches, like the chaffinch, are solitary in the breeding season, keeping to a territory that gives them a steady supply of nutritious caterpillars. They defend this against other chaffinches, because there is only enough food for one family.

Others, like the linnet, are social in summer. They feed on weed seeds, found in few places, but abundant where they occur. Flocks of linnets all find enough to go round.

Greenfinch

Goldfinch

STARTING OUT

WATCHING BIRDS

Already we have seen some of the fascinations that make up the hobby of birdwatching. It is capable of developing into a detailed, lifetime study, or remaining a weekend hobby. It depends on what you want to make it.

Most birdwatchers start because they like birds: they are bright, colourful, cheerful and fascinating. Once they learn more about them, they want to take a deeper interest. Many are content to learn basic identification, so that they can put names to birds they see. Some, the dedicated identification experts, can take this, in itself, to great lengths and an extraordinary degree of sophistication.

Everyone likes to see 'new' birds and the occasional rare bird. Such finds are exciting and add to the enjoyment of birdwatching immensely.

It is possible to enjoy birds without knowing anything about them. But it is much more satisfying to understand something about their ways of life. To

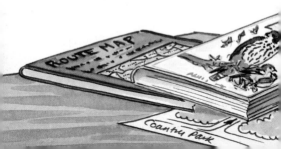

do this, it is necessary to be able to tell them apart: identification is a basic first step.

Detailed study

Identification is not necessarily an end in itself. The long, patient study of individual birds, or particular species, reveals the most remarkable facts. Repeated watching in a particular area – a 'local patch' perhaps – reveals patterns of movement and population changes that can rarely be appreciated in other ways. You can see migration in action and watch the ebb and flow of bird populations over the years.

Birds can be watched, photographed, ringed, tape recorded, or sketched. How you enjoy them is up to you: the only rule for birdwatchers is that the welfare of the bird comes first.

BECOMING A BIRDWATCHER

To put a name to a bird is important, because all your other observations will be pointless if you do not know to which species they refer.

The first requirement is a good identification book, or field guide. These come in all shapes and sizes. Some promise instant, easy recognition: beware! Bird identification has to be learned and comes with experience and practice. You can't expect to play a piano, run a four-minute mile or create a brilliant oil painting without learning how to do it first and then spending many hours practising. It is the same with birdwatching: but the practice is thoroughly enjoyable.

Good field guides have birds painted by an artist. The artist can put all the birds in natural poses, side by side for comparison, in good, even lighting. Photographs need to be used with care, as they may have highlights too pale, shadows too dark. Look at something like the *Collins Field Guide to the Birds of Britain and Europe* by Peterson, Mountfort and Hollom, or *Collins Pocket Guide to the Birds of Britain and Europe with North Africa and the Middle East*, by Heinzel, Fitter and Parslow. Experiment with others later.

Practise makes perfect

Look, read and learn: but most of all, get outside and see real birds. Start near to home, in the garden or park. Then go farther afield: do not be tempted to dive straight in at the deep end and see a whole host of rarities before you even know the common birds close at hand.

Ask other birdwatchers what there is to see and where. Look at local bird club annual bird reports to get the flavour of the birds in your area. Do your homework: it is much better than hoping to be an expert when you only ever watch birds on your annual holiday.

Using a field guide

Use field guides with care. Try to avoid looking at a bird, getting a rough idea of what it looks like, then flicking through the pictures until you see something that is similar. That way, you are bound to make mistakes. Instead, try to be a bit more logical. If you can, learn the characteristics of the basic families from the book, so you can have a good idea, when you see one, whether a bird is a warbler or a finch, a wagtail or a flycatcher. It is good fun and essential background.

Do not go for the nearest colour picture. Remember, your bird might be a female or a winter plumage male, or a juvenile: these plumages might not even be shown in your book. So, use the text as well as the pictures. If there is one, look at the distribution map; the habitat and the time of year when you should expect the bird. If you see something in southern England in winter which should, according to the book, only be found in Scotland in summer, you are probably wrong. It is unlikely that you have found something so outrageously rare right away. Remember that most birds you will see will be common, in exactly the place, habitat and time of year that they should be seen. Take the book with you when you are birdwatching, but concentrate on what you can really see for yourself.

SOUND AND MOTION

Field guides are extremely valuable but they can only show a static, silent bird. For movement, you can go to videos; for sound, use cassettes and compact disks.

Videos are not always very helpful, but the better ones give a good idea of the way the birds look alive and free: how they move, how they stand, even how they sit still. They give a good impression of something that even the best paintings may fail to capture: something birdwatchers call 'jizz'. This is a 'certain something', an indefinable air, the character of the bird, which may be a sum of its plumage patterns, its shape, its motions and behaviour. It is best compared with the character of individual people. How can you tell your family and friends from crowds of people in a shopping centre? It is hard to describe, but you can do it. In the same way, once you know your birds, you will tell them apart, too, by some difficult-to-explain way that comes from their jizz. The only way to reach this stage is through experience.

Using calls

Most birdwatchers locate most birds by sound: they may identify many of them by their sounds, too. Books describe sounds, but one 'tak' sounds much like another 'tok' unless you hear the real thing. Tapes provide a solution. For the best reproductions, compact disks are wonderful: digital stereo sound brings the calls, songs and even the whistle of the wing beats into your living room.

These are great entertainment – you can listen to a singing nightingale in mid winter – but also let you learn the calls and songs of most birds in your own time. It is, however, true to say that the words in a book, the colours on a painting or the sounds on a tape are much harder to remember than the real thing. Only when you see and hear a bird for yourself will it stay forever in your memory.

One of the finest songsters is the nightingale

EQUIPMENT
Choosing binoculars

One piece of equipment almost essential to any birdwatcher is a pair of binoculars: you will be too limited without them. You get more or less what you pay for: they are not cheap but will last a lifetime. Good second-hand ones are less expensive. The highest prices are scarcely justified by relatively slight improvements in performance.

Look for binoculars magnifying between 7 and 10 times – certainly no more. The two figures – 8 x 40, 10 x 40 and so on – indicate the magnification and the diameter of the large lenses in millimetres. Go for 7 x 50, 8 x 30, 8 x 40, 10 x 40 or 10 x 50. Anything bigger will be far to unwieldy, and higher magnifications give too small a field of view and do not focus close enough. With small birds close up, you will often wish you had 7 or 8 when you cannot focus with 10s; but with seabirds, waders and wildfowl at long range you will find 7 too small a magnification. You have to compromise.

The wider the lens the more light the binoculars let in, so the brighter the image. But the binoculars are then bigger and heavier. 'Roof prism' binoculars, with a straight-sided shape, are more efficient than the older type (with stepped sides) so 10 x 40 roof prism may be a better bet than a 10 x 50 conventional pair.

Good binoculars are a joy to use: treat them with care

Using binoculars

Good binoculars are a real joy. To get the best from them, keep them safe and free from bumps and knocks, and the lenses clean.

Look at the focusing wheels. There should be two: one you use all the time, one you set once and then forget (not quite: you should check it now and then to see that it has not moved). The main central wheel focuses on different distances, so you will need to use it to look at birds close up or far away and will constantly move it while following birds in flight. Relax your eyes and let the focusing wheel do the work.

Learn to focus your binoculars as soon as you get them

Adjusting the eyepiece

Before you start you must adjust the individual eyepiece setting. This balances any difference between your eyes: if it is out of adjustment you will see blurred images and get headaches.

Look at a sharp object like a post at a moderate distance. Place a hand or a notebook over the right hand lens and focus with the central wheel, using only your left eye. Then cover the left lens and look with your right eye. Do not touch the middle wheel! Use the individual eyepiece adjustment to focus that eye: first turn it fully one way to get it out of focus, then gently bring it back to the sharpest point.

Now both eyes are balanced and you need not use the eyepiece setting again (but it may turn if it swings against your clothing). Use only the central wheel.

Telescopes – a closer look

Binoculars sometimes do not give enough magnification to let you see birds far out on a lake or across a mud flat. Then, you need a telescope.

Most beginners and many quite expert people do without a telescope. Other beginners proudly carry a new telescope through the depths of a wood, where they will never be able to use it. You can use a telescope in most open spaces and even birds at close range look super through a telescope in giant close-up, but telescopes are most needed when birds are far away.

Most are now 'spotting scopes' or 'field scopes' without telescopic draw tubes. They are solid, quite

A telescope is useful for shy birds or those that live in wide open spaces

short and squat and heavy. The best have lenses at least 60 mm or even 80 mm across and magnify around 20, 30 or 40 times.

Because of their size and shape and the high magnification, they are awkward to use. Old, long ones could be balanced on a knee or gatepost; the new ones are too short and really need a tripod. This is one more heavy item to carry, but it is worthwhile.

As with binoculars, look through a lot of telescopes before you buy one and make sure you can use the one you choose comfortably. It needs a bit of practice, but eventually you will enjoy the good views it gives you.

Angled telescopes

Many telescopes have angled eyepieces. These are harder to use at first, because you look down while the telescope is level or even pointing upwards, so finding the bird is harder. But it is a much more comfortable method when you get used to it. You can stand and look down into the 'scope instead of crouching down and cricking your neck to look 'straight' through it. It is also much better to 'lock on' to a bird and then let the whole family look at it: so long as it is low enough for the shortest person, everyone can use it without adjusting its position.

Care and use of optics

With binoculars and telescopes, never look directly at the sun. Try to keep them dry: most are damp proof but may not be fully waterproof.

If you keep your binoculars in a cold car overnight, take them out of their box before you want to use them, so they do not steam up for the first five minutes when you try to watch birds: you can miss some good opportunities like that!

When you want to look at a bird, do not look down at your binoculars, put them to your eyes and swing them up. Instead, keep your eyes on the bird and swing your binoculars up to your eyes: learn to 'aim' without sweeping your binoculars from side to side trying to pick up the bird in a tree. This is more difficult with telescopes, but the same principal applies.

Without binoculars, birds are often too far off to see well

Binoculars bring birds up close for easier identification

A telescope or larger-magnification binoculars give a bigger image but need brighter light and a stable support

GETTING OUT OF DOORS

Now you have your binoculars, you can get out, or look out of your window, and see some real birds. It may not be so easy as you think!

This is why starting close to home is a good idea. If you go to a remote wood and see nothing but dots in treetops, silhouetted against the sky, and slim shapes disappearing between the leaves, you will risk becoming disheartened before you start.

Mute swans are easy to identify

Using field guides is a special skill in itself. Most books tell you to leave the guides at home and take out a notebook and pencil. This is good practice for note-taking, which is a vital skill, but it may not be the best way to learn your birds. Instead, use the field guide in the field where it is intended to be used. But do not skim it and pick the first bird you come to. Things are almost invariably more complicated than that.

Some birds are easy to identify. A magpie, a mute swan, a kingfisher, a robin – none of these present difficulties. But what, say, of a spotted thrush or a streaky finch? Can you remember what you have to look for? Why not check the book, while you can still see the bird, and make sure that you have seen all the crucial features?

With a thrush you might see the colour of the bill and legs, or note down the pattern on its head: but these will not help. The guide will tell you, instead, to look at the features which distinguish this species: the shape of its spots, the length of its tail, the pattern of its wings. Use the text to make sure that you do not miss problems not necessarily illustrated: are there winter plumages, or special patterns under the wing, or on the spread tail? There is little point in looking at a bird without knowing what characters, or field marks, to look for: so, take the book with you and make sure that you get it right.

Juvenile mistle thrushes look strange and often catch people out

41

KEEPING NOTES

It is best to have a small, field notebook and to copy your notes into a neat version later. People use all kinds of methods: nowadays, many birdwatchers use miniature Dictaphone out of doors and put their notes and lists onto computers at home. Others prefer card indexes.

There is a lot to be said for a straightforward diary, but it has its drawbacks. If you keep a diary-style 'log', you can always refer back to it, years later, and be reminded of great days out, at wonderful places, with amusing and entertaining companions. The diary will have it all there, together with a list of the interesting birds you saw (and their numbers), and descriptions of rare birds, or odd pieces of behaviour.

Cards and computers

If you want to check how many firecrests you have ever seen in your life, it gets difficult after a few years with a diary: you really need a card or a file for firecrest. This is where the computer comes in handy. Yet these files have little else to offer: you cannot get a complete idea of the whole day, or holiday, with all the birds and all the places in one book. You could consider keeping both kinds of logs.

The value of notes goes beyond simple reminiscences. At the end of each year you can pick out all the noteworthy records and send them off to the county recorder: doing your bit to build up the knowledge of local birds and to put something back into your hobby.

Add your own ideas

Your log book can have a good deal of identification information, too. You might like to scribble all over your field guide, or prefer to keep the books neat and tidy and make notes elsewhere. In either case, feel free to note that the book is wrong on this point, the picture too red here, too brown there, or the birds look too fat, too long, too slim.

You will soon want to build up your own identification guidelines and this is a real help. Make notes in the field and, especially, try to make little sketches of birds you see. Even matchsticks and ovals will do. Label the sketch with the colours and patterns: that way, you have to look at every part of the bird and you will not miss anything out. It is hopeless trying to remember later, especially once you have opened a book.

Sending in the evidence

For rarities, especially, the local bird club will want details like this if it is to believe your reports. Unless you can supply some sort of evidence, your rare birds will not be accepted! But taking field notes is great fun and a wonderful discipline: above all, it makes you really look hard, and once you do that, you will begin to remember things without needing to look at a field guide again.

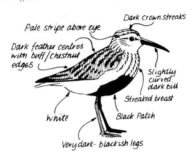

Dark crown streaks

Pale stripe above eye

Dark feather centres with buff/chestnut edges

Slightly curved dark bill

Streaked breast

White

Black Patch

Very dark - blackish legs

The dunlin below is described in the notebook above

Gatherings of birds at feeders give a chance to practise taking notes

MAKING SENSE OF A BIRD

Making notes gets easier after a while. It is not easy to use words that other people will understand, but, for the time being, it is you that must understand them most. If you think a bird is 'slim' and someone else says it is 'fat', do not worry, so long as you know what you mean and can picture it later.

Try to be careful, however, with the descriptions you use. Judging size is extremely difficult: there are some people who say we can only judge size by saying 'it looks as big as the bird that I think it is' – in other words, you have a preconceived notion and do not really get an objective judgement at all. A bird in the sky is a classic example: a swan a long way off looks the same size as a swallow close up. It is really the shape of the swan, its actions, its ponderous wingbeats and the speed of movement against the background that makes you think you can judge its size.

Try to judge size and shape by comparison with other birds that you really know nearby: if there are such birds handy. If you see a new bird on the lawn, you might be able to tell that it was as big as a sparrow or a fraction longer than the starling next to it. Comparison is the basis for a great deal of identification.

Measurements do not always give a good idea of a bird's size and photographs may be misleading: compare the house sparrow (left) with the starling behind it and the closer (apparently much larger) starling to the right

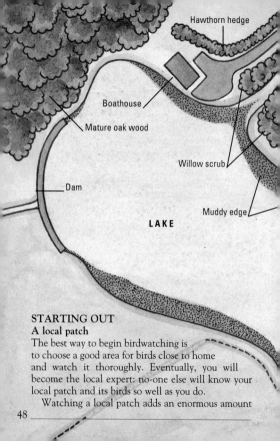

Hawthorn hedge

Boathouse

Mature oak wood

Willow scrub

Dam

Muddy edge

LAKE

STARTING OUT
A local patch
The best way to begin birdwatching is
to choose a good area for birds close to home
and watch it thoroughly. Eventually, you will
become the local expert: no-one else will know your
local patch and its birds so well as you do.

Watching a local patch adds an enormous amount

of extra interest. You can watch bird populations alter with changing habitats: a marsh dries out and you lose some birds but gain others. A patch of scrub gets overgrown and you lose whitethroats but discover blackcaps. The local lake may have no waders one year, but the next, when a long, hot summer means the water level drops and there is a muddy edge, you might find dozens.

Relating changes to different circumstances is fun. Keep a good log and a few sketch maps and it will become fascinating. It will also begin to

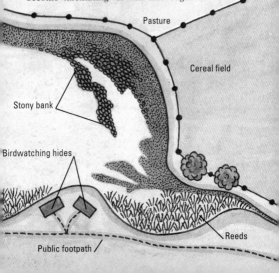

Pasture

Cereal field

Stony bank

Birdwatching hides

Reeds

Public footpath

figure in the local or county bird report: your observations, based on intensive watching year after year, will come to have some significance and real substance.

Semi-tame geese on the park lake may attract wild mallards and tufted ducks

Your local patch will provide many joys. If you go to a wood and see a great spotted woodpecker, it will be good but quite normal. If your local patch has no real trees and you have not seen a woodpecker there for 10 years, but suddenly one turns up, then that same 'normal' great spotted woodpecker becomes a great rarity, a really exciting find!

Watching a local area is full of such surprises. You will discover many things that you did not know existed. Go at different times of the day, even at night, and find that snipe, which you never suspected were there, come to roost in a field, or barn owls, which you had never seen before, appear over a patch of rough grass at dusk. Who knows what you might find?

The kind of birds you see and the potential for greater discoveries depends on where you are, what kind of habitat you are watching and, to some extent, the effort you put into it. Let's look at some examples.

Great spotted woodpeckers may be found in parks and large gardens as well as woodland

How about a rather ordinary patch, inland, without any water? Well, maybe you will find a ditch, or a farm pond, or even a garden pond. Water, always, makes a focus for birds.

Fieldfares eat rotting apples in orchards and can be tempted into gardens with windfalls

Even on dry, cultivated land, you can see migration in action. In the autumn you will have fieldfares and redwings to watch out for: first of all picking berries from the hedges, later pulling worms from the ploughed fields. Even if they do not come to land, migrating gulls, lapwings, starlings and thrushes can be found on the move all over the United Kingdom. In winter, if there is a heavy snowfall, you might see many thousands of them fleeing west, in search of kinder conditions.

In the winter unexpected birds roam around: maybe treecreepers along hedge banks, or reed and corn buntings along the field edges. The sparrow flock may be joined for a day or two by redpolls, linnets or bramblings.

In spring, a wheatear might bob along in front of you across an open field and the first swallow will investigate an old shed or the cricket pavilion. Overhead, kestrels may display; over any decent, dense bit of wood it is worth keeping an eye out for sparrowhawks.

Farmland is the typical habitat of the corn bunting

Bewick's swans
are exciting
visitors from
Siberia in winter

If you can visit a reservoir, lake or flooded gravel pit, so much the better. Suddenly a whole new set of birds is added to those of the trees and dry ground that surround the site.

In winter there will be wildfowl: you might be lucky, especially after cold or rough weather, and spot a local rarity on the move. It could be a smew, or a black-necked grebe, or perhaps a storm-blown kittiwake or a party of Bewick's swans.

By spring, the wildfowl will have paired, great crested grebes will be on eggs, and you will be eager to spot the first sand martins and swallows. The early migrants along the shore might surprise you: the books may say they are resident, but meadow pipits, pied wagtails and reed buntings will all be on the move. Later they are joined by yellow wagtails and then some waders, such as ringed plovers, common sandpipers and dunlins.

Pied wagtails move around a lot and small groups often appear beside lakes and reservoirs at migration times

Autumn is the time for more migrants, moving in a more leisurely fashion, so they often hang around for a few days. You could find common and black terns, greenshanks and ruffs, flocks of swallows and martins. Almost anything can turn up, almost anywhere!

At the coast, if you are fortunate enough to live there, your local patch really could be something special.

Estuaries are among the richest wildlife habitats in the world. The United Kingdom is blessed with more than 150 of them and there are innumerable little bays and inlets, too. Nearly all are good for birds, sometime or another.

Little stints fly south from the Arctic each autumn and some appear in Britain

Rocky coasts have different birds but are still interesting and headlands have added spice in spring and autumn. Here almost any bird might be seen, resting or passing by on migration. Some of the best birdwatching spots in Europe are on the coastal headlands where all kinds of rarities drop in, but the usual fare is an exciting procession of 'common' birds, all year round.

Do not forget, too, that there are birds out at sea. Especially if there is a good wind, particularly an onshore wind, passing seabirds and wildfowl may be brought in close enough to see from the shore. Birdwatchers who can do their patchwork in places such as this are fortunate indeed.

The wryneck is a rare migrant, most often seen near the east coast

IN THE GARDEN

CLOSE TO HOME

There is a great deal to be said for beginning your birdwatching career close to home. It is quick and easy to get to; there is no need to worry about transport, weather, permits, or how to carry food, books, notebooks, binoculars and other gear. Just look out of the window when you feel like it and study the birds in your garden.

This is, of course, a very early stage: you will soon want to go farther afield. Nevertheless, garden bird watching is something you can enjoy for many years to come: the joy of seeing the common, colourful, busy birds of a typical British garden never fades.

Song thrushes are declining but still visit many gardens

GARDENS AND PARKS

If you do not have a garden, then the nearest park, especially with a park lake, is the next best thing. It will, anyway, be the first place to go for the birdwatcher who wants to make a move from the sparrows and blue tits to something more demanding.

A good garden can be enhanced by the provision of

- the right kind of plants (birds like berries, so berried bushes are a good start)
- a feeder (whether a bird table or a simple bag of nuts)
- a nest box
- some water (a pond, or a bird bath).

The next few pages deal with common garden birds and the simplest ways to provide what they need: which means they are more likely to come to you.

Classic peanut-eaters
include the blue tit

GARDEN BIRDS

Garden birds are surprisingly varied. Much depends on the locality: in Scotland there will be no nuthatches or willow tits, but there might be other specialities instead. A lot also depends on the size and nature of the garden and house, too.

Older houses, especially those built between the wars, often have open eaves which allow access for swifts. Newer ones have no swifts (a real problem for the long-term future of these birds) but smart, new, white eaves attract house martins. Few houses nowadays have owls in the roof, but a good many have collared doves singing from the television aerial.

Collared doves are widespread and common. Their strong, rhythmic trisyllabic 'coo' may wake people up at unearthly hours but can be comforting and evocative. Despite their abundance, collared doves were unknown in the UK until the mid 1950s, when they reached here after a dramatic spread across Europe from Turkey.

Collared doves
are common
suburban birds

Usually only larger gardens attract other pigeons, but wood pigeons, shy on farmland (where they are shot), may be bolder in the suburbs and come to take berries from ivy and elder, or leaves from your peas and beans. They are wonderfully attractive at close range.

Magpies are the bane of many garden birdwatchers, as they do take a number of eggs and chicks of smaller songbirds. Yet that is their natural way of life: and, undeniably, they are extraordinarily handsome, and clever, birds.

Magpies are familiar in most suburban and rural areas

Much more typical of our 'ideal' garden bird is the robin: tame, confident, a bossy and aggressive resident with a fascinating lifestyle. The dunnock is much less obvious, apparently quiet and demure, yet its social life involves complicated relationships. The robin has the better song: a lovely, flowing warble with a particularly wistful air in autumn, while the dunnock's song is faster, less varied and a little flatter in quality.

SUPERB SONGSTERS

Thrushes are frequent in gardens, particularly in the form of the song thrush and blackbird. Song thrushes are neat, rather small, clean-looking thrushes with pale creamy breasts closely spotted with dark brown. They are responsible for smacking snails against stones of patio slabs, leaving heaps of broken shells as tell-tale evidence.

Blackbirds are larger and bolder; the males are coal-black with vivid yellow beaks, while females are dark brown, somewhat spotted on the throat but never so pale as a song thrush. Juveniles are redder, and more spotted, but always darker than other thrushes and with dark legs (song thrushes have pink legs).

Broken snail shells beside a stone or slab give away the presence of a song thrush

Song thrushes have a magnificent song: it is easily told by the habit of repeating most phrases two or three times. These phrases are very varied, with some harsh, throaty notes and fast rattles, but many are of the purest and strongest quality, almost unbelievably intense on spring evenings. Blackbird song is a more fluent, relaxed performance, without the instant repetition, but has a gloriously musical, fluted quality that few songsters equal.

Much more gregarious, lively and excitable than the blackbird is the starling: a longer-legged, shorter-tailed, squabbling busybody which looks black with creamy speckles in winter and a more solidly dark colour in summer, with iridescent reflec-tions of green and purple. Starlings are typical bird table birds and they soon empty a bird bath with their energetic splashing.

Starlings are under-rated and deserve more admiration

GARDEN ACROBATS

Another group of typical garden birds is the tit family. Most gardens have blue tits and almost as many see great tits at least occasionally.

Blue tits are small, bright, acrobatic creatures that can hang upside down or sideways. They are recognised by their blue, green and yellow colours, with a blue cap above a white face. In gardens near to woods, there may be 10 or 15 at a time: but the true total during a whole day may be several times that number!

Great tits are bigger and slightly less agile; they have glossy black heads with bold, pure white cheeks and a broad black stripe down the middle of the yellow breast. If the stripe widens out between the legs, it is a male; if it tapers away almost to nothing, it is a female. The males with the broadest stripes are the dominant ones, likely to rear the most young.

Larger than a blue tit, the great tit is slightly less agile

Coal tits are frequent garden birds near wooded areas. They are less easy to watch as they tend to steal a peanut and make off with it, rather than eating it on the spot. They lack any green, blue or yellow, but look very neat in black, white, grey and buff. Look for the two white bars across each wing and an oblong white patch at the back of the head.

Coal tits are smaller than blue tits and remarkably quick and light in their actions

Willow and marsh tits are also duller, brown, buff and black tits, with large black caps and small black bibs. The willow tit is a richer colour beneath, looks less tidy around the head and has a pale panel in the wing, whereas the marsh tit is paler, neater and glossy-headed. If the bird calls a strident 'pich-yoo!' it is a marsh tit. These two are less commonly seen than the others in gardens.

Peanut feeders

To attract more tits, put up some simple feeders. Peanuts are irresistible to them, but you can experiment with all kinds of other foods (so long as you avoid desiccated coconut and long bacon rinds). Peanuts are prone to a fungal infection which is deadly to birds, so be careful to buy 'safe nuts' from an approved dealer within the Bird Foods Standards Association.

The feeder can be a simple plastic mesh bag (as good as anything, but short-lived), a wire mesh basket (be careful not to let rotten nuts collect at the bottom) or a much more sophisticated device designed to keep out sparrows and squirrels while letting the more attractive blue and great tits in to feed.

Put nuts out all winter. If you wish, do so in spring, too, as the birds will not feed such unnatural food to their chicks unless there is a complete failure of the caterpillar harvest.

In spring, peanuts may well attract tiny, delightful finches called siskins. These are lovely, agile birds, with sharp, triangular beaks and forked tails. Males are vivid green and yellow with black caps and streaks, while females are greenish, almost white below, with fine streaks. They are predominantly birds of the north, liking pine forests best, and many of our garden siskins are from far off parts of the Continent. They feed on peanuts in spring when their natural food is scarce.

Make sure that feeders are not too close together, so that more birds can feed without fighting, and make sure they are not close to a nest box if you would like it to be used by nesting birds, as they prefer peace and quiet away from the hubbub at the feeder.

Siskins are most frequent in gardens in spring, when natural foods are scarce

House sparrows try anything and soon learn to cling to a feeder

Varied fare

Food can also be put out regularly on bird tables. A table can be a simple board slung beneath a branch, or even on a bracket under a windowsill. it is usually best placed on top of a smooth (preferably cat-proof) post. A roof may keep birds away at first, and does little except keep food dry in the worst wet weather, but you might like a roof for decoration.

Do not buy a bird table with a 'bird house' on top. The nest box is sure to be too small and the wrong shape, and nesting birds simply do not get on with those that are fighting to get a turn at the food.

Be inventive with your feeding. Rotten apples are excellent in winter, attracting blackbirds, other thrushes and starlings. Fill the skins with bread and milk, or mixed seeds.

To help birds such as wrens and dunnocks, which do not come to feeders, scatter bits of cheese and finely-grated scraps under bushes. Fat and cheese smeared onto tree bark attracts treecreepers and woodpeckers. Lumps of suet and uncooked pastry may bring in great spotted woodpeckers from nearby woods.

Make 'bird puddings' with scraps from the kitchen, seeds, peanuts, dried berries and fruit, mixed in with warm, soft fat and left to solidify in convenient containers (such as yoghurt pots). Put a piece of string in before it goes solid and you can hang up the mixture from the bird table or a tree.

Many species of bird are not likely to be helped by peanuts or kitchen scraps in baskets. Instead, we can help to supply extra natural (or semi-natural) food.

Great favourites are berries: good, rich, juicy packages of pure energy. The best are often cotoneasters and rowan berries, but not all varieties are eaten with equal enthusiasm. Often pyracantha berries are greedily consumed but sometimes they are left untouched all winter: but then, in early spring, they can be a lifeline when other food is in short supply.

Other berries are good, too: deep, purple-blue berberis fruits attract young blackbirds and starlings in late summer. Greenfinches devour the berries of mezereon even before they are ripe in late spring. Elder fruits, beautiful in spreading clusters of shiny purple-black berries in August, are superb for unlikely garden visitors, such as blackcaps, garden warblers and lesser whitethroats and these same birds may visit to take advantage of a fresh crop of red honeysuckle berries.

▲ Blackbirds are
great berry-eaters

▶ The mistle thrush is
less regular in smaller
gardens but comes in
for a feast of berries

Apart from berries, crab apples are adored by mistle thrushes and blackbirds: and any of these fruits, in a rare winter with an influx from Scandinavia, might attract a waxwing.

Native shrubs are often said to be best for garden birds and certainly hawthorn, rowan and elder are excellent. Nevertheless, the ornamental ones such as cotoneasters provide good feeding and, when it comes to nest sites, even the oft-criticised ornamental conifers have much to offer.

Nesting birds need good, thick cover, away from the eyes of magpies and thieving cats and squirrels. In the early spring, most deciduous shrubs are far too thin and spindly, or still leafless, to provide such cover and a decent conifer may be just the thing to entice an early-nesting blackbird or song thrush. Nothing suits a dunnock better than an old-fashioned and out-of-favour privet hedge.

You can also encourage birds by providing more food: planting buddleias, sedums and michaelmas daisies will bring in more flies, hoverflies and bees and this in turn attracts insectivorous birds.

Buddleia and other plants attract insects which in turn bring in more birds

UBIQUITOUS SPARROWS

House sparrows are generally common, occasionally abundant, but subject to unexplained recent declines in some gardens. They are always bold and confident, but rarely especially tame: often they will fly off at the first hint of disturbance, although they are quick to return.

A house sparrow feeds its chick

Males have grey crowns, edged with rusty-red, and black bibs. The female is duller and browner, streaked with yellow-buff on top, but completely plain greyish-buff underneath, unlike any finch or bunting (but beware the dullest young or female greenfinch which can look quite similar).

Sparrows are not finches, but they have similar triangular, seed-cracking bills. The true finches are a mixed lot but several species are quite at home in gardens. Of all of them, the goldfinch is the prettiest, with a striking red, black and white head and black wings crossed by a broad band of yellow. Goldfinches are seed-eaters, preferring thistles, dandelions and teasels, and they do not care much for bird feeders in gardens. Instead, they come in to take advantage of large, leafy, airy ornamental trees like planes and limes, in which they often nest.

The best way to attract them closer is to make a small pond and watch for them to come and drink and bathe. Sparrows do the same: in fact, they are among the most energetic of visitors to the bird bath or pond, and they love to dust bathe, too, creating unwelcome hollows in flower beds in summer dry spells.

Tree sparrows are neater and more handsome than house sparrows; they have become scarce in recent years. This one is dustbathing

73

FINCHES

The chaffinch is a common garden bird, especially in the north and west. Males are pink beneath, browner on top, with a blue-grey cap and blue bill in summer (in winter these colours are duller). Females are a nondescript greyish-olive colour, paler below. Look for the white sides to the tail and two bands of white across the wing on all chaffinches. The upper wing bar is often hidden by overlapping feathers, but flashes brightly in flight.

Greenfinches visit gardens when natural supplies of seeds and berries run low

Redpolls have increased in suburban regions with plenty of tall trees

Greenfinches have yellow on their wings and when they fly off show large triangles of yellow each side of the tail. Males are vivid apple-green, with greyer wings, but females in winter can be quite dull, looking very dowdy on a grey day. Look for the deep, pale pink bill and an angry frown created by a dark 'mask' between the eyes.

Chaffinches feed on the ground or on a bird table, but greenfinches love to hang on peanut feeders, or to feed greedily on cotoneaster berries. Also on peanuts, especially in red bags, tiny, delicate siskins appear, especially in spring. Redpolls are also small, short-billed finches, but streaky brown, with a dark red cap and tiny black chin. They do not visit bird feeders, but often fly over suburban gardens making trilling calls, probably nesting somewhere near in a dense hawthorn or ornamental conifer.

Swifts

Young swallow

Swallow

SWIFTS, SWALLOWS AND MARTINS

Birds of the air above the garden, rather than in the garden itself, are the swift, swallow and house martin. Swifts are larger than the others with longer, slimmer, scythe-like wings. They look all black-brown, flying around in flocks high in the sky in late summer, screaming loudly. Swifts arrive in May and leave in August; they nest in hidden hollows under eaves and in church towers. House martins are very different: they are the small, fluttery black and white birds that make round 'mud pie' nests on the outside of a wall up against the eaves, often on new houses. In flight they are easily told by their all-white underside and a broad

House
martin

House martins build the
familiar mud cups under
eaves

white patch on the lower back. The best way to
encourage martins is to make sure there is some mud
for them in spring, so that they can build their nests
afresh.

Swallows are much more elegant and supple,
seeming to flow through the air, often low to the
ground. They need more open space because they
hunt low down instead of above roof height, so
gardens rarely have them. Swallows are steely-blue,
with long, forked tails, deep red on the throat and
creamy, pale orange undersides. They nest inside
outhouses, car ports and old sheds, putting their
saucer-like nests on top of a ledge or beam.

BOXING CLEVER

Nest boxes in gardens help many birds to find a safe site to nest and also allow us to get a good, intimate view of their family lives.

The standard wooden box suitable for blue tits needs to be bigger than most people think, so the chicks cannot jump out of the opening before they are ready. The hole should be at least 12 cm from the floor; the box at least 15 by 15 cm inside and 20 cm deep at the front.

Put the box out of reach of cats, if you can, and away from a bird table: there is no point in attracting birds to a box if they are continually trying to drive off birds attracted to food alongside. If you have an average sized garden, one box is plenty: do not put too many close together, as you will again have several pairs constantly fighting each other and in the end all will give up and go away.

Alternative designs

Be adventurous with nest boxes. You can even buy or make artificial house martin nests, which may serve to start a new colony: make sure they are not over a window or porch where the droppings will be an annoyance.

Open-fronted boxes allow quite different kinds of birds a chance to nest. Robins, wagtails and flycatchers all prefer an open box to one with a small, round

hole. Make a standard sized box but with the top half of the front cut away. Put it in a deep, shady recess or inside a thick conifer for robins, which like peace, quiet and security.

A shallower box, even half a coconut, will do better for spotted flycatchers, which like to be able to look out as they sit on their eggs. Put the box in creepers on a wall or trellis, or alongside the overgrown trunk of an old apple tree. Do not expect instant occupation though: it may take years for spotted flycatchers to find it.

Starlings are common enough in gardens, but you might like to build a large box, 30 cm tall, 20 by 20 cm wide, with a 50 mm hole in the front, for them to nest in. House sparrows may well take it over, but there will be some lively scraps over who has the right to settle in it if it is in a good spot.

Even bigger boxes may attract woodpeckers, but it is a rare garden that has such splendid birds within it. Most people will be content with a pair of blue or great tits and a pair of robins.

House sparrows will take over a box if the entrance hole is large enough

Nest boxes may attract some very unusual birds: in this case a kestrel

A tree sparrow using a nest box

Making a nest box

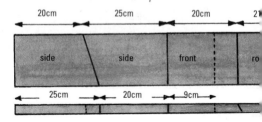

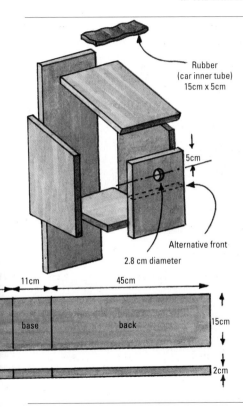

Rubber
(car inner tube)
15cm x 5cm

5cm

Alternative front

2.8 cm diameter

11cm

45cm

base

back

15cm

2cm

DRINKING AND BATHING

Water in the garden has already been mentioned as a major attraction for birds.

Birds need water, even in the dead of winter. On a freezing day, flocks of starlings will descend and splash about so vigorously that a small bird bath will quickly be emptied. They need to bathe to keep their feathers in good order, especially in cold weather when good insulation is vital.

Starlings, more than most birds, demonstrate the need for water all year round by vigorous bathing

Almost any kind of receptacle will do for a bird bath: as with most bird garden equipment, simplicity is a good byword

A pond, a sunken dustbin lid, a small plastic drip tray, or a concrete bird bath, all do the same job. The birds drink, too, and clean, fresh water is essential for their well-being. Fill the bird bath regularly and keep it clean and free from droppings and general mess. In winter, try to keep it clear of ice, but never add anything to stop the water freezing: it may poison the birds.

CREATING A POND

A good garden pond will probably be at least a metre across, with a deep end and a shallow end with some bare gravel so that small birds can bathe and drink.

Dig out a good-sized hole, deeper and larger than the final pool. Line it with thick butyl, or concrete. Then put in a layer of earth or gravel and, if you wish, add a few pond plants from the local garden centre. Decorate it with some stones and gnarled old boughs – these also act as good perches for birds (as well as dragonflies and frogs).

Fill the pool gently with a hose and, if you can, add some water from a clean natural pond or canal. You might like to get some frogspawn from the pond of a neighbour. The birds will come themselves: especially if you sit quietly out of sight indoors, watching patiently. You might even like to build a hide and try to photograph your visitors.

1

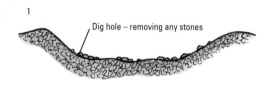

Dig hole – removing any stones

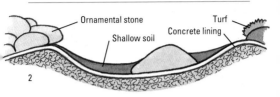

Ornamental stone

Turf

Concrete lining

Shallow soil

2

Hose pipe – Fill gently to avoid eroding pond soil

3

GARDEN BIRD COUNT

The British Trust for Ornithology runs a long-standing garden bird survey and would welcome your help in adding counts. It is a simple thing, just totting up the birds you see during an hour or so, at intervals during the year.

You can do your own counts and keep records of what you see and when. Once your knowledge increases, you can take note of the age and sex of birds like blue and great tits and work out which are the highest in the pecking order, if any. Which species dominate at the feeder? Does any particular individual seem to be the overall boss? Do the numbers change week by week, or the proportions of males and females and immatures?

UK Top 10 garden birds (early 1990s survey)

1. Starling	6. Robin
2. House sparrow	7. Great tit
3. Chaffinch	8. Greenfinch
4. Blue tit	9. Carrion crow
5. Blackbird	10. Magpie

Unless you are a licensed ringer and can mark the birds individually, there is a limit to what you can do. It is generally impossible to tell even how many birds use your garden in a day: there might be ten times as many blue tits as you think. It is also, as a rule, impossible to tell an individual bird from one year to the next. Many people talk fondly of 'their' robin, a friend for years, but probably have different robins each year, all of which learn to come to take food. Others have 'old blackbirds' and 'the blue tit with the bent tail', but, in reality, such birds cannot be recognised year after year – bent tails, especially, will not last long, but blue tits often bend them as they sit in a nest box for hours on end.

Great tits, being larger and more aggressive, get the better of blue tits but avoid fighting by using threatening postures

THE TOWN PARK

A perfect place to see more variety than in the average garden, yet still have some familiar and approachable birds to study, is a town park.

A good-sized park with a mixture of lawns, shrubberies, flowerbeds, trees and, especially, a lake, should prove worth watching all year round: and not just for the beginner. Park birds will give enjoyment for years to come.

Town and country pigeons

Town birds include pigeons. The familiar street or park pigeon is a descendent of the wild rock dove, first domesticated (as homing and dovecot varieties) then gone wild again. There are now countless generations of 'feral pigeons' as they are known (literally 'gone wild') which can be almost any colour but typically revert back to the blue-grey wild type.

Wood pigeons are large, handsome birds and add colour to a town park

Wood pigeons are bigger, with broad white wing and neck patches and they have never been domesticated. They are big, beautiful pigeons with lovely, subtle colours and the classic, soporific multisyllablic dove coo. Collared doves are everywhere: pale sandy-grey birds with a thin black collar and black and white undersides to their tails. They have a loud, abrupt triple coo, like 'cu-cooo-cuk'. Their spread across Europe from Turkey this century has been one of the great natural changes in bird distribution and no-one really knows why it happened.

Other birds in town parks include the greenfinch where there are dense shrubs, and the nuthatch, but only when there are big, mature broad-leaved trees (especially beech, limes and sycamores). These are woodland birds that survive well in a suburban environment which still has a woodland element.

Domesticated pigeons, kept for homing or for food, are descendants of wild rock doves. Escaped pigeons have colonised most towns

CREEPING IN THE SHRUBBERIES

Around the edges of flowerbeds and shrubberies, the dunnock creeps and shuffles quietly about. It rarely makes much fuss although it has a penetrating whistle and a shrill, fast, warbling song. It looks rather dull, brown and grey, but it has very complicated social relationships.

Another quiet, dull bird of the park edge, although up in the branches of trees, on fences or walls rather than on the ground, is the spotted flycatcher. Dull in colour, it is bright and alert in behaviour, look-ing intently for flying insects which it snaps up in a mid-air foray. It is a late arrival from Africa, rarely appearing before mid May.

Bigger park birds include the mistle thrush, which nests very early high in leafless trees, but may dive-bomb intruders with a noisy, dry, rattling call. In the autumn it quickly strips rowans and hawthorns of their berries. Jackdaws are small crows, pigeon-sized and slaty-grey rather than inky black. They are intelligent and fascinating to watch. They nest in church towers and other old buildings and inside hollow trees. Magpies make big, round, roofed fortress nests of thick sticks in dense bushes and often enter parks on the look out for scraps.

Dense shrubbery, especially with plenty of evergreens, attracts blackcaps, small warblers with a rich, fast-flowing song. They are primarily summer visitors, but more and more spend the winter in Britain, especially where they have access to food on bird tables. Taller, leafier trees with more air and light are needed for goldfinches, which love planes and sycamores and come down to feed at low level on the seeds of thistles, dandelions and related plants.

Wrens inhabit the same sort of places as dunnocks, foraging at low level, in the dark, cobweby places under shrubs and beside ivy-grown walls. They often jump out and chide an intruder with quick, chattering scolds before diving back into cover, or fly up to a higher perch and deliver a sudden outpouring of loud, rich, fast song, always with a flat trill in the middle.

◀ This brown-eyed, grey-faced, streaky bird is a dunnock

▶ Jackdaws are widespread birds of towns, cliffs and quarries

THE PARK LAKE

If the park has a lake there may be moorhens, dark birds with a white line along each flank and big white feathers under their tail which can be flirted in anger

or alarm. Adults have a wonderful sheen to their plumage and an unreal sealing-wax red and yellow bill. If they walk out of the water, as they often do to feed, you will see their big feet, with very long, thin toes.

Park lakes are excellent places for learning to recognise common birds and seeing them at close range

Mute swans are familiar birds of even small ponds, unmistakable with their knobbed bills and long, sinuous necks. Canada geese like big pools with easy access to areas of short grass, where they graze and leave copious droppings. They were originally brought to Britain as ornamental birds and spread to many lakes and parks: their brown plumage with a black neck and white chinstrap makes them easy to identify.

The classic park duck is the mallard: the one with a loud, vulgar quack (only from the female, in fact). Males are bottle-green on the head with a white collar, females bright brown with darker speckles. Both have a purple-blue wing patch edged with white and vivid orange legs. All kinds of farmyard derivatives have gone back to the wild, so many town mallards have curious, sometimes ugly, black, khaki, cream and white varieties: the pure wild birds are certainly the most handsome.

Coots prefer to stay on the water while their relatives, the moorhens, are more often on land or at least in the vegetation at the edge of a lake. Coots are rounder-backed, bigger-headed birds, without the cocked and flirted tail of a moorhen. They are also all slaty-black, except for a big white shield on the face and white bill. Their feet are also huge, but the toes are broadly lobed.

Moorhens are generally shy but are often bolder on a park lake

Winter wildfowl

If the lake is quite big it may attract a variety of ducks. Deeper water brings in diving ducks, especially tufted ducks and pochards. Tufteds are neat, round-headed birds, the males beautifully black and white with a droopy crest, females dark brown with a trace of a tuft. They dive constantly, just disappearing from view under the water. Pochards tend to be much more sleepy by day, feeding mostly at night. Males are pale grey with black at both ends and rich, chestnut red heads, while females are duller, browner and show only an echo of the same pattern.

Tufted ducks are the commonest ducks, after mallards, on town ponds

Pochards feed at night and spend most of the day asleep

At the edge of the lake there is often a small, slim, lively bird running and walking about, frequently on tarmac or concrete rather than flowerbed soil. This is the pied wagtail. It does wag its tail – or, more accurately, bob it up and down – all the time as it runs and skips about, frequently making short flights in pursuit of insects. Its black and white or sooty grey and white plumage and long tail make it an easy one to spot.

Beside a few park lakes in autumn and winter grey wagtails may appear. They are supremely elegant, the longest-tailed of all the wagtails and with the most exaggerated, swinging tail wag. All ages and sexes, all year, have a blue-grey back, a black tail with white sides and a greenish-yellow rump, and underneath the tail is a splash of deep yellow. In summer, males are yellow underneath except for a glossy black bib. They are shyer than pied wagtails and frequently take flight as someone enters the park, usually with a sharp, thin 'chik' or 'chissik' call.

A grey wagtail may visit a park pond, especially in autumn and winter

City gulls

Most obvious in winter, flying about or swimming on the lake, or just loafing around on jetties and buoys, black-headed gulls are by far the most likely gulls to be found. They are small, very white, in winter with just a black ear spot on the head. In spring, the head turns dark brown (with a white forehead at first). Red legs are a giveaway, as is the triangle of white on the leading edge of each wing.

A little larger and darker, with dull greenish bill and legs (never red) is the common gull. In winter it has a dark, streaky head and the back and wings are darker than a black-headed's, the wing tips tipped black and white. While black-headed gulls chatter and whine, common gulls have a particularly peevish, high, thin squeal. Both are adept at diving for scraps and chasing others until they can steal a morsel of food.

Gulls are now found almost everywhere: black-headed gulls are most common

FARMLAND

Farmland encompasses two main types of habitat: arable (ploughed, seeded and harvested) land and pasture, upon which livestock is grazed.

Farmland birdwatching is sometimes more productive than watching birds in parks and gardens, although the birds are often less approachable and more difficult to find. The open countryside does, however, have more to offer in terms of variety and especially in the change of bird populations from season to season. Getting out into the countryside gives you the chance to appreciate bird migration much more fully (see pp.208-221): and there is also a bigger conservation job to do here, as the study of bird populations on farmland is vitally important in monitoring the changes brought about by new agricultural practices.

There are well under 5000 pairs of barn owls remaining in Britain

A large proportion of our barn owl population still nests in old barns

Farmer's friend

Several 'typical farmland birds' have declined to a frightening extent in recent years. Barn owls have disappeared most obviously from many regions. They like rough grazing, where voles abound, but such unkempt areas are few and far between in intensively farmed landscapes. The owls have also suffered from the loss of old barns and ruinous outbuildings and the destruction of old hedgerow trees. The cavities in buildings and trees are crucial to barn owl survival as they nest, roost and rest in them and need several per territory. Watch likely places at dusk in summer and in the daytime on very cold winter days, when the owls may hunt during the short daylight hours.

Little owls like farmland and parkland, where plenty of trees survive. They may be seen sitting quietly in trees by day and can be heard at dusk, making loud, clear whistling calls. As they fly, you will see a distinctive swooping, switchback action recalling a woodpecker.

THE USEFUL HEDGEROW

Farmland with hedges is best for many birds. Once the hedgerows are destroyed, and especially if the taller trees are cleared, some species disappear. Tree sparrows are finding survival difficult in places. They need tree holes for nesting, and like stubble and weedy fields for winter feeding, but with winter cereals sown in clinically-clean fields they simply cannot feed. The same goes for lapwing flocks (once so familiar but driven from many places, perhaps by too liberal an application of pesticides which destroy the soil's invertebrate population) for corn buntings (which like the declining barley but dislike increasing winter wheat) and linnets (which struggle once straggly, thorny hedges are grubbed up and winter stubble ploughed in).

Whitethroats are summer visitors which prefer rough, uncut hedges and lesser whitethroats like the really big, ancient hedgerows with thickets of hawthorn and blackthorn. Prairie cereal farms lack both of these warblers.

Kestrels are typical of farmland, hovering over roadside verges (often the only rough ground, with voles, that is left) or sitting on poles and wires hunting by carefully watching for movement. People still call them 'sparrowhawks' but kestrels are really quite different from the elusive, woodland-edge hawks which would never sit in the open on a telegraph pole or wire and which never hover.

Stock doves are hole nesters, like kestrels and several owls, so they need big trees or owl buildings. They are doing well in parkland but declining in intensively farmed areas. Turtle doves are certainly seriously on the wane. They feed in late summer stubble but in spring prefer rambling, overgrown hedges and the edges of woods. They are also suffering greatly from illegal shooting on the Continent.

Bluer, rounder and smaller than the wood pigeon, the stock dove is a handsome farmland bird

A small hedgerow bird that may also be seen at peanut feeders in gardens is the willow tit. The closely similar marsh tit is more of a woodland species: in a thick hawthorn hedge, or a willow and thorn thicket at the corner of a field, a black-capped, brown tit is most likely a willow.

Willow warblers, which arrive in April, are also hedge birds if there are sufficient tall bushes and trees scattered through the hedgerow. They have one of the most exquisite of all spring bird songs. They do breed and feed in willows close to lakes and streams, but are not specially linked with willow trees in general.

Red-legged partridges were originally introduced to the UK from southern Europe

A brace of partridges

Two gamebirds are very much linked with arable fields and old meadows: the grey partridge and the red-legged partridge. Both feed on grains of all kinds but require an abundance of insects if their chicks are to survive: hence spraying of insecticides has caused a massive decline in recent decades. Red-legs like drier, sandier soils and may often be much more obvious than greys, marching boldly across ploughed ground in small groups and even perching on top of haystacks and barns. Grey partridges tend to be more secretive, but their odd, creaky calls give them away on summer evenings.

A small falcon, the hobby feeds on dragonflies and small birds

The increasing hobby

Apart from kestrels, one other falcon is a true farmland bird although it has long been associated more particularly with heaths: the hobby. It seems that hobbies have been overlooked in many areas, but they are clearly increasing in some. They breed in old crow's nests in tall trees, often in a spinney of pines or at the edge of a big plantation. They nest in June and July, when they can be extremely elusive, although they may be more easily seen in September, when they chase martins and wagtails as they gather to roost in reeds each evening.

A domed fortress

Tall hedges and isolated trees often have the fortress nests of magpies in them, most obvious in winter: these are big, black bundles of sticks with a domed roof. Magpies have recently increased to a more natural level after the reduction in persecution and poisoning by pesticides, although farmers and gamekeepers now trap thousands each year. They are spectacular, intelligent, fascinating birds, a typical part of the English countryside (far less common in Scotland) but unwelcome in most people's gardens. Unfortunately for them, their liking for baby songbirds is often very public, unlike the secretive and more damaging depredations of cats.

Magpies make strong nests of thick sticks, often in the middle of thorny thickets.

Pheasants creep out of woods and hedges to feed on fields but most are now reared and released for shooting and relatively few are truly 'wild'. They were introduced to Britain long ago, but still look spectacular and a cock pheasant at close range is a delight.

Other farmland birds that rely on hedges and trees for some sort of cover, be it for nesting or as a safe retreat all year round, include the blackbird (such a familiar garden bird, but equally a farmland specialist), the mistle thrush and various finches and buntings. Greenfinches, for example, feed in tight, coordinated flocks all winter in weedy fields.

The declining lark

Skylarks breed in open fields, nesting on the ground in short vegetation or on ploughed land. In some parts of England they have declined to a sad remnant of previous numbers, a real loss for those who enjoy the sparkling outpouring of a lark overhead in spring: its song is one of the most remarkable of all. They actually avoid hedges and even feed away in the open, where they have a good view of approaching danger.

Skylarks are best known for their stream of continuous song

ROAMING THE FIELDS

Open fields attract flocks of lapwings, especially on damp meadows and recently ploughed ground. With them (often on ancient, traditional meadows) golden plovers may be found. In some places they spend the winter, while some favoured fields see flocks each spring, when they are gathering prior to a return to their breeding grounds and look their best in handsome breeding plumage.

Hedgerows add an important wildlife habitat to farmland

Also roaming the fields in winter, frequently flying up to the tops of trees if disturbed, are flocks of fieldfares and redwings. Unlike the tight-packed bands of small finches, these form loose aggregations although they often behave in a well coordinated way. They are great worm-eaters, hopping about over fields, sometimes in the company of blackbirds (at the field edge), larks and lapwings.

As well as black-headed gulls, which feed almost anywhere, common gulls visit the fields in winter, especially short grass on which they can search for worms and grubs. Bigger gulls tend to feed elsewhere and use open fields simply as loafing areas, passing away spare hours before flying off to roost, but common and black-headeds are true farmland feeders.

In the winter, too, roaming bands of long-tailed tits can be seen in the hedges, groups of yellowhammers in stubble and along the field edge (always within easy reach of cover in case a passing sparrowhawk should appear), flocks of chaffinches (sometimes with bramblings mixed in) and, of course, great gatherings of rooks.

Rookeries are characteristic features of the British and Irish landscape

Rooks are superb birds of farmland: they breed and roost in tall trees but move out in great flocks each morning to the fields, where they plod about all day long in search of worms and grain. With them may be smaller, jauntier, greyer birds – jackdaws. Carrion crows tend to be less social, but may roost in large numbers together and sometimes gather in flocks on fields that have been treated with manure.

WATER – MAGNETIC ATTRACTION

Farmland floods, much reduced from the days when most lowland fields flooded every winter, attract birds in abundance. In really rainy weather it is often well worth seeking out some flooded fields for particular attention.

Water on farmland is a great attraction to many kinds of birds

There will always be gulls, especially black-headed (common too, in places, but they are far less evenly spread) but you might be surprised at what else you see. Look out for moorhens, coming from secret places in ditches and beside farm ponds to enjoy greater freedom on the flood; snipe, which revel in the watery ooze and sticky mud into which they can probe with their long, sensitive bills, and redshanks, which are sporadic visitors to most farmland but may pause for a day or two after rain.

Ducks will certainly include mallards, but floods
might attract a small band of teals or wigeons for a day
or two, and in the south, especially, Bewick's swans
sometimes investigate a flooded field or wet meadow.
Special floods on nature reserves in the Fens and
elsewhere attract hundreds, even thousands, of these
wild swans which come from Siberia each winter. Few
birds are more romantic and awe-inspiring.

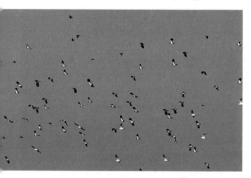

Lapwings fly in flocks from as early as May until late winter

Mute swans also paddle about and waddle out of
the water onto wet meadows. They are far less
comfortable on land than the smaller, more agile
Bewick's swans; while in the north, other, bigger wild
swans, whooper swans, are also more at home on dry
land than the heavy mutes.

THE LOST FARM POND

Farm ponds used to be the focus of much wildlife in farmland, from frogs to dragonflies. Now, however, ponds are hard to find: and so are the frogs. The birds have gone, too, from the corners of fields where moorhens and kingfishers could be seen in little oases of green, undisturbed water.

Moorhens like small areas of water – ponds and ditches as well as rivers

If you find a pond, it is worth watching, and probably worth preserving. There should be moorhens: these nest at the water's edge and particularly like a spot where an overhanging or broken branch dips its twigs into the pond. Mallards will probably find even the smallest pond, while teals and tufted ducks require rather larger patches of water.

At the edge, snipe feed and, if there is a dark, overhung, muddy place which you can watch secretly and quietly from a distance, you might catch a glimpse of the deep-bodied but slim-shouldered form of a water rail.

The true value of a pond is seen in summer, when all manner of birds and other animals come to drink. Swallows also feed over the pond and together with house martins use its margin to gather balls of mud, with which they build their nests. A farm pond is an excellent place to erect a hide, from which to watch or to try your hand at some bird photography.

Swallows may suffer poor nesting seasons in very dry summers: they need a supply of mud for their nests

FRESHWATER

FRESHWATER SITES

There are relatively few natural lakes in southern Britain; those of the Lake District and Scotland are mostly large, cold and deep with less obvious vegetation around them and fewer birds than rich, shallow lowland lakes.

Reed- or sedge-fringed lakes are good for great crested grebes, which need such vegetation to which they anchor their nests in spring. Little grebes are content with smaller pools.

A reed-fringed lake has special birds such as reed and sedge warblers

Grey herons nest in trees, often away from water, but feed at the water's edge. Shallow lakes with plenty of eels, other small fish and frogs are ideal. They are shy but easily seen, so watch from a distance as they patiently search for fish.

Ducks are a mixed bunch, with surface-feeders (or dabblers), some of which also graze on dry land, and diving ducks the obvious groups. Mallards are everywhere; teal breed beside much wilder lakes, often high in the hills or in boggy sedge-beds alongside acid lakes in the north. Tufted ducks and pochards are the commonest diving ducks.

If there is a grassy area, or swampy fields grazed by cows, beside the lake, yellow wagtails are likely in summer and early autumn (although not in the far north). They like wet places, especially where cattle stir up flies from old cow-pats: these are good wagtail food.

Yellow wagtails require damp pasture land with plenty of insects

Many sheltered lakes have mute swans: in some places there are sizeable flocks of birds, which are mostly immature, non-breeding ones. Where a pair settles to nest, they will drive away intruding swans and keep an exclusive territory of their own. You may often see old nests – huge heaps of waterweed and reed stems – right through the winter. Whooper swans visit lakes in Wales and northern England and many Scottish lochs. They are winter visitors from Iceland and much wilder than mutes, distinguished by their straighter necks and yellow and black bills.

Shovelers like shallow, lowland lakes with a rich food supply suspended in a real 'pea soup'. They use their unique, spatulate bills to sieve out the tiny animal life. Gadwalls are neater, smaller-billed ducks and have taken to eating food brought up from the bottom by diving coots.

The splendid fisher

Lakes are naturally good spots to look for kingfishers, but many are too open and exposed. The kingfisher likes some shelter and prefers to hide away in overhanging trees or in secluded bays and the mouths of inflowing streams. You will hear more than you see: listen for a shrill, penetrating whistle, often with a 'catch' in it: 'keee' or 'ch-keee'. Occasionally a kingfisher will fish in a more open spot by hovering, rather than perching, to search for prey.

Kingfishers are colourful but difficult to see and smaller than many people imagine (not much bigger than a sparrow)

RESERVOIRS

Reservoirs are much the same as natural lakes in many respects and some newer lowland ones, which have flooded productive farmland, have a burst of new life for several years before 'settling down' with fewer birds. If the water level falls in spring and summer, the muddy edges become overgrown; with rising water levels in winter, the seeds of the waterside plants are released into the water, making splendid conditions for teal, wigeon, mallards, shovelers and Canada geese.

Reservoirs attract many species but concrete shores have a limited appeal

When the water level falls late in the summer, in a dry spell, the reservoir edge becomes a perfect spot for migrating waders which pause to feed on the mud.

Most common inland are dunlins, ringed plovers, ruffs, redshanks and common sandpipers. Watch for green sandpipers in muddy creeks, greenshanks on more open banks and snipe in really wet, oozy mud. If you can make regular visits – daily if possible – you will find an enormous amount of movement as waders come and go, numbers fluctuating almost by the hour. There is a good chance, too, of a rarity turning up.

On the water you should see cormorants – more common now than a few years ago – as well as more ducks in winter, such as goldeneyes, goosanders and ruddy ducks. It is also quite likely that there will be some semi-tame Canada and greylag geese about, but a much more exciting find, in November perhaps, would be a group of migrating Bewick's swans. These small, stocky, musical swans are visitors from northern Siberia.

Redshanks often feed beside reservoirs where the shores are muddy

GRAVEL PITS

Gravel pits are often flooded after being worked out and they provide excellent habitats for birds. Their edges are often quite steep-sided and sand or gravel is not much good for waders, so these birds are often limited in number and variety. Redshanks are most likely. However, great flocks of tufted ducks and pochards are often found, with goldeneyes from about October to April. Look among them for oddities: in winter there might be a scaup or a long-tailed duck; in autumn or spring, a black-necked grebe. In the south you may be lucky enough to find a beautiful smew.

Gravel pits add areas of water to otherwise dry landscapes, but suffer from a lack of oozy mud

In early spring the first summer migrants will usually be sand martins (which nest in the earth banks) and little ringed plovers (small waders which nest on disturbed ground, often worked out sand pits). If there are willows along the water's edge, there should be chiffchaffs by the end of March, too, while swallows feed over the water by mid-April.

A little later, common terns will probably call in on migration. If there is a gravelly island (or a specially-provided artificial raft) they will settle to nest.

'Waste' areas alongside the pits attract a variety of birds, often not normally associated with water: stock doves, red-legged partridges, migrant wheatears and whinchats, pied wagtails and reed buntings. If you have a rough, wild gravel pit close to home, you are lucky: take full advantage of it.

Sand martins tunnel into vertical earth banks to nest

WOODLAND

BIRDS AND WOODS

Most people with little knowledge of birds tend to think that they are usually found in trees: a 'typical' bird might be expected to be found sitting on a branch, singing. In fact, birdwatching in woods is often quite difficult. In autumn, you could be forgiven for thinking that there were no birds at all in most woods!

Oak woods contain some of the richest bird and insect populations in the UK

In winter, woods are pretty empty until dusk, when birds flock to them to spend the night in relatively warm, sheltered conditions. With the burst of new life every spring, as leaves appear and caterpillars are abundant, dozens of birds can be seen, all singing and fighting for territories, later finding food for their young. Usually they are spread out evenly through the wood (although the edge is always best) because each pair has its exclusive patch, or territory. By autumn, the young birds have flown and it is better for birds to be together: many pairs of eyes are better than one when it comes to spotting predators, or finding food. It is then that the woods seem empty most of the time, until you come across a wandering feeding flock: suddenly there will be scores of birds of several kinds, all roaming about together.

The best way to birdwatch in a wood is to walk slowly and quietly with frequent long pauses to look and listen. Use your ears, especially – you will need to stop to listen properly. Then, if you find something, sit quietly and be patient. Once you find a mixed flock in autumn or winter, stick with it: get around in front, if you can, and let the birds stream past you. They often seem oblivious to your presence and come extremely close, which is one of the special joys of woodland birdwatching.

Nuthatches are essentially birds of deciduous woods with mature trees

DECIDUOUS WOODLAND

What birds you can expect depends on the season, the place and the kind of trees. Deciduous woods in summer are rich and productive, but vary greatly from region to region. Typical southern, lowland woods with a lot of oak, holly, cherry and sycamore will have plenty of common birds, from tawny owls (hard to find) and woodpeckers to blackcaps and chiffchaffs.

Coppiced woodland creates a dense habitat ideally suited to some warblers and nightingales

Tall, closed woods tend to have tits, warblers and thrushes, as well as wrens and dunnocks, rather than finches or buntings (which like more open spaces). Great spotted woodpeckers are common, lesser spotted scarce and hard to see (listen for their high, peevish 'pee-pee-pee-pee' notes), while green woodpeckers prefer much more open woods and heaths.

Light at the edges

It is the woodland edge and clearings that let in sunlight and create greater variety: in fact in most places, the edge of a habitat, where two or three habitat types meet, will always be the best for birds. A woodland edge, beside a lake or a heath, will be wonderful.

In summer (not before mid May) look for spotted flycatchers. They often spin out from perches high in the trees, to snap up a fly and then return to the same twig. Garden warblers sing from rather bushy undergrowth or the middle level, blackcaps (which sound very similar, equally beautiful but with a sudden outburst in the middle of the shorter song) frequently from higher up or amongst rhododendrons and hollies. Chiffchaffs sing their name from the treetops. Willow warblers are more edge birds, often found in bushy places and beside overgrown footpaths rather than deep in woods.

From the depths of the densest undergrowth, in southern Britain, listen for nightingales in May and June. They are wonderful singers, often active by day but best heard at dusk and dawn.

Blackcaps live in woods with plentiful, dense undergrowth

The woods are home to rooks which make big, stick nests in colonies right at the treetops. They feed, though, out in open fields. Jackdaws may nest with them or in old trees with big holes, which may also be home for tawny owls. It is best to listen for tawny owls at dusk (often hooting but equally often giving a loud, whining 'ke-wick' note), but you might find one by following up the noise made by a 'mobbing' party of small birds which have found an owl at roost by day.

Woodland predators

Sparrowhawks are woodland predators but you rarely see them inside woods. They slip through at speed, silent and elusive. It is best to get back out of the wood and look over the top in spring, when the sparrowhawks fly up into clear air to display. Buzzards do the same and are also best seen from outside the wood, rather than from under the trees.

Woodcocks are special woodland birds, related to the waders of muddy shorelines but living in damp, soft leaf

The woodcock is a worm-eater of the woodland floor

mould and overgrown ditches. They nest on the woodland floor, where they are virtually invisible, but come out at dusk through the summer to fly over the treetops in regular circuits, giving sharp, high whistles and deep, frog-like croaks as they go. A woodcock watch is likely to be good for owls, foxes and even badgers, too.

The dawn chorus

Typical songbirds in the wood include robins and chaffinches, song thrushes and blackbirds. Go at dawn to listen to them sing: it is an experience that everyone should share as often as possible. The late spring, deciduous woodland dawn chorus is one of the great wonders of birdlife in Britain.

Autumn flocks

In autumn, the deciduous woods are more open and easier to watch but the birds are more often gathered together in flocks. The high, thin, colourless 'zee-zee-zee' sounds of long-tailed tits are quite different (with practice) from the richer, more emphatic 'zee-zee-zee' sounds of goldcrests. Blue tits give similar little squeaks and trills and are often abundant, frequently turning somersaults at the very ends of twigs, while the bigger, heavier, less acrobatic great tits like the

bigger branches and even feed a good deal on the floor. Beech trees often produce great crops of mast and great tits feed on this with chaffinches and nuthatches. Marsh tits love beech trees, too, often acting much the same as great tits, while coal tits are even smaller and lighter than blue tits and equally acrobatic.

Long-tailed tits roam woodland edges and hedgerows in large family groups

Creepers

Treecreepers have another version of the 'zee-zee' theme (more like 'seee-seeee' and very thin), which you will soon learn to recognise. They are forever climbing trees, making their living searching out tiny creatures in the bark. Nuthatches are more mobile, bobbing about and climbing up and down, over and under, using their strong feet. Treecreepers use their stiff tails, too, as supports, and do not come down the tree head-first.

Jays are active and very obvious in autumn as they fly about, collecting acorns and taking them off to bury them, ready for eating in the winter and next spring.

Few birds are so constantly restricted in their habitat as the treecreeper, which clambers up tree trunks all year round

WINTER WOODLANDS

In winter the deciduous wood can seem cold and dreary but a fine, sunny day reveals a wealth of life still finding a suitable niche within the trees.

Woodpeckers can be active and obvious: they drum (a short, rapid burst of sound) only in spring, but all year round their loud tapping against branches gives them away. Beware: nuthatches and great tits tap vigorously too.

The chaffinches under beech trees may be joined by bramblings (winter visitors from Scandinavia) while seeding beeches and hornbeams are the best places to look for the scarce and elusive hawfinch. Many birdwatchers take years to see a hawfinch and the first one is an exciting achievement! Often they sit at the very tops of tall trees, like stocky, rounded fir cones unexpectedly stuck on bare branches. If they are disturbed (all too easy) they go off with a sharp, robin-like 'tik'.

Bramblings are very closely related to chaffinches and the two often mix in winter

This is a good time, too, to walk through the brambles and dense ground layer in the hope of disturbing a woodcock or two. They get up at your feet and go off with a fast, zigzag flight, with a loud burst of whirring wing-noise. They are nothing, though, to the more likely find of a pheasant, which will burst up when you least expect it with a great clatter and loud crow, testing the nerve of any birdwatcher.

Pheasants are glorious creatures when seen at close range

A SCATTER OF CONIFERS

Mixed woods naturally add a few more ingredients to the recipe for woodland birds, with holly, a few larches, pines and spruces all bringing in something extra. In summer, these are good for coal tits and goldcrests and in a few favoured places even firecrests.

Late in the summer, little patches of spruce or pine may have crossbills, too, which sometimes swarm out of the Continental conifer forests and roam west in search of food. Their loud 'chip-chip-chip' notes draw attention to them, but beware of confusion with young greenfinches in late summer, which sound rather similar.

Woodland is the favoured habitat of many familiar garden birds

Flash of white

The bullfinch is a typical bird of the edge of a wood, mixed with thickets and hedgerows and a variety of shrubs. It is not always shy but usually quiet and secretive, so easy to overlook. You might see little more than a sudden flash of a broad, white rump as it (or more often a pair) fly into the depths of the thicket, usually giving a low, fluty pipe as they go. If you can, follow them, carefully and quietly, for a bullfinch is a joy to behold: the male is a glorious bird of blue-black, blue-grey and rich red-pink.

Bullfinches are relatively scarce in gardens and mostly remain around the edges of woods and in thick hedgerows

Chaffinches take to mixed woods well, as they are equally at home in dense conifers and open oaks. They are territorial and sing a lot in spring, but in winter flock together in the fields or under sheltered spinneys.

BEECH WOOD SPECIALS

Beech woods have already been mentioned and are rather special. They have big, high-crowned, dense-canopied trees that spread together to shield the ground from sunlight and prevent much in the way of undergrowth beneath. This excludes a good many birds that need bushy growth and dense vegetation at ground level – anything that likes to poke about in a bramble bush (like a wren) or hop under the overhanging leaves of an elder (like a dunnock) is out of luck in a beech wood.

Instead there are a few birds that prefer dense leafy trees high up, but open spaces underneath. One is the wood warbler. It skips about the canopy in late spring and early summer, the males frequently pausing to sing with a passionate, liquid 'pew pew pew' or a loud, ticking trill that quickens to a silvery shrilling like some sort of cricket – 'ti-ti-tickikikirrrrr'.

Beech woods have little undergrowth in their dense shade: some species, such as wood warblers, prefer this

Wood warblers nest on the ground, preferring a sloping bank with a dense covering of leaf litter, although many nest near a broken or drooping branch which gives a sheltered 'ladder' down to ground level from the high canopy where they feed.

Redstarts breed in holes in the trees although as a rule beech trees are not well-provided with cavities. Nuthatches, however, also find the odd hole (often a woodpecker hole) and plaster around the entrance with mud to reassure themselves that the opening is just the right size (even if it was already about perfect). Nuthatches are never more at home than in a beech wood with plentiful large, smooth boles and heavy horizontal branches.

Redstarts do not make their own holes but need a ready-made cavity to nest in

WESTERN OAK WOODS

Western oak woods are quite different from the oaks of lowland England. Here there are sessile oaks; tall, slender trees when full-grown, but often stunted and twisted and covered in a wonderfully rich growth of lichens. The ground below, often sloping and rocky, is usually overgrazed by sheep, so there are few young trees and little undergrowth.

Western oak woods are beautiful places, with old, gnarled trees and plenty of open space on the forest floor

Wood warblers are perfectly at home here, too, as the dense canopy and open ground layer are the same as in beech woods. Redstarts find many more holes in the gnarled oaks and can fly out to feed on the edges of rough, bushy slopes.

This pied flycatcher is in a natural hole, but many nest in artificial boxes

More confined to these western oak woods are pied flycatchers. They nest in holes, too, and feed on insects caught in the open beneath the trees. They often hunt at the edge of a sunny space. All three – wood warbler, redstart and pied flycatcher – are best detected by hearing them sing. Learn their songs from a tape in the winter before making an expedition at the end of April.

Tawny owls are common here, as are sparrowhawks, while buzzards are typical of the wooded valleys of Devon, Wales and south-west Scotland. In mid Wales, the very much rarer red kite nests in oaks but feeds over open moorland and farmland.

In the bottom of the valley there is usually a clear, tumbling stream, which is the place to look for dippers. Dippers are found in a variety of waterside places, but only at the water's edge: they are as confined to the water as a treecreeper is to the bark of a tree. Dippers are like giant black and white wrens, which bob and dip at the waterside and suddenly dive in, or walk deliberately into the stream, where they feed on bottom-living insects such as caddis fly larvae.

Where the river broadens into a more open reach, with shingle banks, common sandpipers are likely: they are there from about April to August. Like the pied flycatchers, redstarts and wood warblers, which disappear from the dark green woods of late summer,

the sandpipers are quickly gone after they have nested and a late summer visit to these valleys will often leave a birdwatcher disappointed.

In winter the woods are often devoid of life unless you can find a roaming band of blue, great, marsh and willow tits, perhaps with a treecreeper or woodpecker tagging along. Sparrowhawks still hunt the valleys and this is the best time to look for kites, when there is no fear of disturbance. Besides, they are easier to see then, floating over the hillsides and careering down to feed on a dead rabbit or to dispute the ownership of some edible scrap with a buzzard or a flock of crows.

▲ Common sandpipers nest near stony lake shores and beside clean, shingly rivers

◀ Welsh valleys have a fine mixture of habitats, from open hill and crag to woods and streams

LARCH WOODS

Larch woods are among the most delicately beautiful of all woodland types, with their fresh, vivid green foliage in spring, the sweeps and curves of their long, drooping branches and their golden-yellow autumn colours.

They are home to some interesting birds, although nothing that cannot be found elsewhere: but larch plantations, especially mature ones, are worth exploring. Redpolls are frequent breeders here and often fly overhead with alternating hard, stuttering calls and higher, ringing trills. In autumn and winter, especially, larch woods in the south attract siskins too, often mixing with redpoll flocks. Unlike some other finches, such as chaffinches (which tend to react separately and move around in an uncoordinated way) these small, active birds move in packs, zooming out of one tree top all at once before bounding off for the next quiet feeding session. Know their calls and you will find many more of them.

Crossbills inhabit conifer plantations and clumps of ancient pines

One other special finch of larch woods is the crossbill: it often feeds on seeds from larch cones, as well as spruce. There are bound to be blue and great tits in larch woods, but this is the place to seek out coal tits: listen for their particularly strong, squeaky, high-pitched calls.

Sparrowhawks often nest in conifers but hunt out in more open places

At night you may see tawny owls, but the typical predator of a larch wood is the sparrowhawk. Find a good spot overlooking an extensive tract of conifers in spring and sit and watch on a clear, fine day: the sparrowhawks (and buzzards, in the west) are sure to appear in their courtship and territorial display flights.

THE PINE FORESTS

Pine forests vary according to their origin, location and age and, of course, the species of tree. Most are planted and vast tracts of woodland are of uniform age, the trees all planted in straight lines. In many areas the oldest forestry plantations are being clear felled, leaving rough clearings, but the best ones for birds are where clearings (including those created by strong winds) are mixed through forests of varying age.

Capercaillies prefer ancient pines with plenty of heather and bilberry underneath

The crossbill is the bird most suited to pines (or, more particularly, spruces) and it is found increasingly where good crops of ripe seed are to be had. It is still erratic in many areas, appearing when the breeding season elsewhere has been good and the birds have moved off in search of food supplies: then any pine wood may attract them.

Great tits, coal tits, goldcrests and treecreepers are typical of these big woods. In the north, the

siskin is more common, but still elusive in summer, and is a real treat worth searching for.

Crested tits chip out nest holes in rotten stumps

Scottish pinewoods

In Scotland there are more ancient, genuinely native woods of Scots pine and juniper with a ground layer of bilberry and heather. These remnants are magnificent and have rare birds: capercaillies (giant forest grouse), black grouse at the edges, Scottish crossbills (big-billed, fat-cheeked crossbills, the only species unique to Britain) and crested tits are among them. Crested tits often forage in treetops and out in smaller pines at the woodland edge – listen for their rhythmic, purring trills.

Special places like this – big, wild woods – may even have breeding ospreys and golden eagles, but buzzards and sparrowhawks are much more likely.

NEW PLANTATIONS

Young plantations on moorland, while destroying moorland habitats, create new opportunities for birds. Most will be common ones – robins, chaffinches, great tits, dunnocks – but some benefit significantly from the tracts of young conifers.

In uplands areas there will be whinchats and stonechats and, later, when there are taller trees beside clearings, tree pipits. Redpolls like plantations when the trees are still barely head-height.

In very young trees, in the north, short-eared owls may nest: they often hunt by day, floating buoyantly over the moors like giant moths. Hen harriers also nest in plantations, especially in south-west and western Scotland.

Young conifer plantations attract whinchats, pipits and short-eared owls

Hen harriers nest in young plantations but are excluded once the trees become too dense

In special circumstances in the south of Britain, especially in the Brecklands of East Anglia, young plantations and cleared areas bring in two rare breeding birds: the nightjar and the woodlark. Both sing at night, but the woodlark is best seen by day. It feeds on open, sandy areas with short grass and sings from a tree or in a circling flight, with a lovely, fluty song. The nightjar begins active life after dark, when its prolonged purring trill or churr carries a long way on a still summer night.

HEATHLAND

LOWLAND HEATH

Lowland heaths are rare and restricted nowadays, although they were once extensive over the sandy wastes of southern Britain and around the East Anglian coasts.

Southern heathland is scarce and fragile, easily damaged by development

They are rare, too, on the continent, so our remaining scraps take on a special value. They support rare plants and exciting reptiles as well as moths and dragonflies to excite the all-round naturalist, but their birds are relatively few in number and variety. What they have are good ones, though.

In summer, look for hobbies hunting over the heaths, chasing dragonflies, swallows and small birds like pipits. They are supremely elegant, acrobatic falcons, but shy and elusive. Another speciality is the Dartford warbler, a little mite with a long, often cocked, tail. It is very dark, with a deep purple-red breast and loves the mixture of low, tight gorse and bushy heather that the best heaths provide. It stays all year in a small area but, should there be snow or ice, the numbers plummet in winter. The Dartford warbler is particularly hard to find, but listen for its soft, purring call, almost a buzz more than a churr.

Dartford warblers remain all year in southern England

There used to be red-backed shrikes on these heaths but they are now gone as a breeding bird from Britain – one of very few recent losses. Summer on the heaths, with the scent of gorse and the colour of various heathers still to come, is good for yellowhammers, linnets, meadow pipits and – in the wake of the pipits – cuckoos.

On heathland, within reach of conifers or mixed woods, you will often flush a green woodpecker. If you take it by surprise it will probably fly off with deep, shooting undulations and a loud, ringing call of alarm, like a maniacal laugh. These woodpeckers frequently feed on the ground, on ants.

Woodlarks breed on a few heaths, too: in the Brecks they like clearings in plantations, but in the south they prefer lawns grazed by ponies and open spaces with sandy tracks. Tree pipits, which are sometimes confused with the larks but are really quite different (slim, longer-tailed, with a buzzy 'teez' call and an altogether different song) are common in summer. Only the meadow pipit stays all winter.

Woodlarks live in clear-felled forestry areas in East Anglia but on heaths and pastures in the New Forest

Linnets are typical of gorsy heaths. They used to be abundant and, in places, are still common, but have gone from many areas where once they were regular. Males in spring sport vivid crimson breast and crown patches and sing well.

Bushy spots have willow warblers and whitethroats: although both are still more or less everywhere, they are showing signs of decline. Nothing can beat the first song in spring from a freshly-arrived willow warbler, an inimitable, sweet, lazy trickle of notes descending the scale.

The whitethroat likes a low tangle of brambles, nettles and thorn bushes

HEATH IN WINTER

In winter, these lowland heaths are dark, bleak places. There may be Dartford warblers to find, but they are hard to catch sight of in dull, cold conditions which make them hide away deep in the vegetation. More likely, there will be a few meadow pipits and the occasional skylark, while overhead the ubiquitous kestrel will still hover while searching for voles.

Winter brings silence to many heaths, with birds few and far between

The great grey shrike is an erratic autumn and winter visitor from the continent. Shrikes are exciting, always alert and imposing despite being only the size of a thrush. Great greys impale beetles and voles on hawthorns in the famous 'butcher bird's larder'. In the 1970s and 1980s great grey shrikes were relatively frequent, but now they have become real rarities.

Birch scrub and scattered young conifers are worked by roaming, nomad bands of tits, including long-tailed tits which stream from bush to bush one or two at a time, making it easy to count their flocks. In the evening, these same places, or patches of taller trees, attract redwings, fieldfares and blackbirds to roost and some are regular roost sites for carrion crows and jackdaws.

Meadow pipits are widespread in all kinds of open places

MARITIME HEATH

The heathland beside coastal cliffs is a special case: like other lowland heaths it has a mixture of heathers, low grasses and gorse, but it is often windswept and very exposed. It is, however, usually free of frost in winter and that makes it a real boon to the stonechat, which often survives hard winters only in these mild coastal places.

Some heaths, especially on the headlands of Wales, still have foraging parties of choughs. These ebullient, likeable crows, which feed on insects, are scarce and entirely western in their distribution. As the coastal heath, on which they rely so much (especially for

ants) has been ploughed up and turned into fields, so the chough has retreated: it has long since gone from south-west England. Linnets love these windy, open maritime heaths, as do yellowhammers which sing all day long, all summer through. Late in the summer, most things are quiet but the yellowhammer still asks for its 'little bit of bread and no cheese' over and over again from the top of a gorse bush or a dry-stone wall.

You never know what might turn up, anywhere, but coastal heaths are good spots for rare birds. In spring and autumn you might find a dotterel resting on migration, a red-throated pipit, or a wandering hoopoe.

▶ Linnets nest in gorse and other isolated bushy clumps

◀ Coastal heaths above the cliffs of south-west England and Wales have been restricted by the spread of farmland

UPLAND HEATH

Heathland going uphill is a little different, often colder, wetter, more likely to be grown over by bracken and have a scattering of larches or hawthorns. It spills over into what is normally thought of as moorland, which is really just heathland higher up the hill (or farther north, where the same conditions are found down to sea level).

Peat bogs and damp heath on hills have altogether different birds from the dry, lowland heath

Here there are many of the same species as lower down – yellowhammers, linnets, sometimes whinchats and wheatears – but a few others too. If there is a good growth of tall heather, expect red grouse. These are not just there to be shot at: they are wild birds and every bit as attractive and fascinating as any other, with one of the most evocative bird calls of all – a loud, staccato, throaty 'kw-arr-rrk-k-k-k-kak-gobak-gobak gobak!'

Scattered trees add black grouse, too, in a few and declining number of places, and carrion crows nest in these trees and leave behind old, stick nests which may be occupied by merlins or long-eared owls. Meadow pipits and skylarks provide food for the dashing little merlins. Kestrels are still the most common raptors, although, if you are close to wooded countryside, expect the buzzard to be more obvious.

Red grouse thrive in a mixture of tall, old heather and fresh new growth

UPLAND

ONTO THE MOORS

In Wales the upland fringe and even the open moor high on the hill is patrolled by the majestic red kite: as splendid a bird as you could wish to meet and one with a fascinating history. Once nearly exterminated from Britain, the Welsh population has, with protection, risen again to a healthier 100 pairs (which sounds a lot, but would make a pretty average crowd at a bird club lecture).

Ravens are the world's biggest crows

The moors in late summer and autumn are also visited by great bands of rooks and starlings which feed on the open slopes, often wheeling about and heading back for the lowland farms if disturbed. More at home here are ravens: occasionally you might come upon a group or even a decent flock of them, but usually you see them in pairs. They are big, handsome crows with the most remarkable abilities in the air. They are the only birds you can normally expect to see roll upside down in mid flight.

CRAGS AND ROCKS

On open ground with a mixture of rocks, scree and close-cropped grass wheatears breed. They arrive in March and leave in late summer: identify them when they fly ahead, by their brilliant white rumps and black 'T' shape on the tip of the tail.

Wheatears are widespread on migration but always close to rocks and areas of grass when nesting

Scree and crags attract another summer visitor that arrives in March – one that is unfamiliar to most people. It is the ring ouzel, a blackbird-like thrush with a chacking, fieldfare-like call and a long-winged, square-tailed shape more like a mistle thrush. Males have a broad crescent of pure white across the chest. Ring ouzels are adept at slipping out of sight just over the next rise – and the next, and the next.

Where the scree steepens to cliffs, stock doves find places to nest on hidden ledges and inside deep cavities. These are usually thought of as birds of lowland farms and parks, but are equally at home on inland cliffs, in quarries and beside the coast.

Ring ouzels are essentially birds of rocky upland slopes with scattered heather and bracken

Peregrines nest on larger cliffs. These falcons were once seriously endangered, in the 'pesticide era' of the 1960s, but are now thriving. They take many feral pigeons as well as other medium-sized birds, which they catch in mid air. They are specially protected and are best sought outside the breeding season: anyone disturbing them at the nest may be liable to prosecution.

Fortunately the decline of the peregrine during the 1960s has been reversed by the ban on persistent pesticides

TAKE CARE ON THE HILLS

Hill walking in search of these special upland birds –
buzzards, harriers, merlins, peregrines, ring ouzels,
grouse and so on – is fraught with potential dangers
and not to be undertaken lightly. Even the Army gets
into trouble sometimes, so don't go out on your
birdwatching manoeuvres if the weather is likely to
turn nasty (and it can, with little warning).

Tell people where you are going, take food and
drink and plenty of warm, waterproof clothing. The
precautions are just as necessary on the south-western
moors and the hills of mid Wales as on the peaks of
Snowdonia and Scotland. In Scotland, of course,
there is the extra temptation to get even higher and
more remote to seek out special mountain-top birds

Only on the highest mountains and most exposed northern hills of Scotland can ptarmigan be found

like dotterels, ptarmigan and snow buntings. They are marvellous, enjoyable birds, but do remember that many are under pressure from people in the most popular sites and that you will be exposed to some of the worst weather in the world if it turns really bad.

Ptarmigan are the most likely of these specialities to be found. They are lovely, doe-eyed, fluffy-footed grouse that turn white in winter and seem so unconcerned that they allow people almost to stroke them before scooting away across the gravel and boulders. Everyone ought to see one, once.

◄ Many parts of northern and western Britain experience weather conditions that can be dangerous

UPLAND LAKES

There are often small (and in places, even large) lakes on the high hills and people often expect them to be full of exciting birds of remote places. In fact, the opposite is usually the case.

Although beautiful to look at, most upland lakes have few birds

These lakes are usually deep, cold and acidic and have little vegetation, so little in the way of food or cover for birds. The pebbly shores are usually bleak and exposed and attract very little beyond the occasional wandering dipper or common sandpiper. In winter, they may have a few goldeneyes and maybe a family of whooper swans on them, but they are essentially rather uninteresting.

Scottish lochs at lower altitudes are often similar, but common sandpipers are more regularly seen on their edges and, if the valley is boggy, perhaps greenshanks, too. These days they are worth scanning in the hope of seeing a fishing osprey.

Divers inhabit some of the lochs. The bigger lochs with islands have black-throated divers, which often fish in the loch that they nest beside. Smaller lochs, sometimes tiny moorland pools, have red-throated divers, which generally fly off to the nearest bit of sea to feed. Both are shy and easily disturbed and best watched with care from a distance, preferably in late summer when they have already hatched their eggs.

Red-throated divers nest on small lochs but feed at sea

LOWLAND LOCHS

Some of the lowland lochs in Scotland are much richer for birds: it is usually easy to tell which because you can see the greater amount of vegetation growing in the shallows.

Black-necked grebes are rare breeding birds in the UK

These often have colonies of black-headed, and sometimes common, gulls. Few situations have so much life, noise and general activity as a gull colony in full swing and they are worth going to see.

Great crested and little grebes may nest in the south but the special grebes of Scotland are black-necked (very rare, only in certain nature reserves) and Slavonian grebes (almost as rare and equally vulnerable). In autumn and winter, the lochs are much more lively, with visiting goosanders, goldeneyes and tufted ducks and, in many cases, night-time roosts of pink-footed and greylag geese. The geese, winter visitors from Iceland, are among the finest of wildlife spectacles and the larger roosts, as at Loch Leven and Loch of Strathbeg, are simply breathtaking.

Golden-yellow 'horns' identify a Slavonian grebe in summer

THE COAST

The coast of Britain and Ireland presents a convoluted, richly varied wonderland for birds. No other country in Europe has such a splendid coastline for wildlife.

Coastal habitats are very diverse and it is essential to find the right kind of place, at the right time of year, to see the birds at their best. In the north and west, especially, but also in some notable east coast sites, the shoreline is hard and rocky, with sheer cliffs, often above a flat, wave-swept sill. In other areas the land lies lower but the hard rocks still create resistant, unyielding surfaces with rock pools and barnacle-encrusted boulders, banks of seaweed and mussel beds. In such places, the birds are quite different from those of sheer cliffs or the softer coast which predominates in the south and east.

British coasts are among the most dramatic and most diverse in Europe

Soft coasts – mud, sand and marsh – are vital for many wading birds

The low-lying coastline in areas where the rock is less resistant is equally varied, with shingle ridges, sandy beaches, extensive mud flats, sand dunes, deeply incised creeks in green salt marshes, brackish lagoons or shallow estuaries. Often in such places the effects of the season and, especially, the state of the tide, will influence your birdwatching.

Seabirds – the species that live their lives out in the ocean – have to come to land to breed, and the coasts of Britain offer a multitude of opportunities. Waders – birds of shallow water and mud – breed in the north but must migrate south every autumn. Again, our shores provide them with their needs until the following spring. And wildfowl – the ducks, swans and geese – flock to the salt marshes and lagoons in their thousands, having flown westwards to escape the severities of a continental winter.

ESTUARIES

Estuaries are frequently misunderstood and misrepresented as bleak, muddy places that are there to be drained and developed. True, birdwatching on an estuary can be difficult: the distances are often vast and the weather unkind. Yet the birds are there by the thousand and an estuary is biologically one of the richest places on earth.

Millions of tiny creatures in the mud feed thousands of birds. Here you will see oystercatchers on the higher mussel scarps; curlews probing deeply for lugworms; bar-tailed godwits probing for smaller worms at lesser depth. Knots feed in dense packs, picking food from close to the surface, while dunlins patter over the mud taking tiny snails and other minutiae.

The curlew's bill looks fragile but is capable of breaking crabs

Alternative strategies

Grey plovers defend winter feeding territories; redshanks feed in the salt marsh creeks and close to cover; ringed plovers like the firmer sand, while sanderlings run along at the water's edge, picking up what is beached or exposed by breaking waves. Then there are turnstones on the pebbly parts, moving seaweed and shingle aside in their search for sandhoppers and beach fleas.

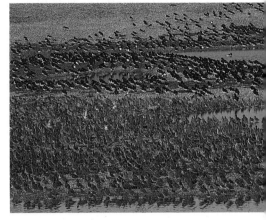

When the tide is high, waders collect together at a safe roosting place

The waders all have their particular place and learning about them and how they feed gives you a better chance of seeing them well. It also shows just how vital their habitat is: no wader can survive without the precise conditions that it needs for feeding and roosting.

On an estuary there will usually be a higher sandbank
that is left dry by all but the higher tides, or is the last
bit of land to be covered as the tide rises. Here the
birds will gather in large flocks on the rising tide,
whatever the time of day: birdwatching is not tied to
time, but to tide.

Often the waders arrange themselves in groups,
species by species, and sometimes you can see the
same species, in the same places, year after year after
year. Oystercatchers settle down into long, black and
white lines, after much jostling and noisy shuffling,
when their vivid orange beaks show to perfection. The
redshanks may be in a quite separate line, while
curlews string out along the water's edge and
gradually merge into the godwits.

Knots are particularly likely to form dense packs when resting

Clouds of knots

Knots are classic estuary birds because they need more open space, larger areas of mud, than the average narrow beach can provide. You may find a few here and there on other beaches, but it is the major estuaries such as the Wash and Morecambe Bay that hold the great majority. As the tide rises they collect into dense carpets of birds and if they are disturbed they fly around in swirling flocks, like clouds of smoke. No birds are so dramatic as these. When the water recedes, so they spread out to feed on the exposed mud, but they still form bigger, tighter groups than the smaller dunlins.

Estuary wildfowl

There are, of course, many other estuary birds apart from the waders. Here there will be shelducks: big, bold black and white ducks with the forepart of the body ringed by a broad orange band. The males have shiny red beaks with big knobs at their base – so vivid as to seem almost unreal. They feed on tiny snails by sweeping sideways with their bills, leaving a strange pattern of fan-shaped curves as they advance across the mud.

Brent geese also feed on the muddy shores, eating eel-grass and algae, but they also come up to the salt marsh and its creeks and, increasingly, to the farmers' fields just inland. They are small, dark geese with the whole head, neck and breast dull black except for a small half-collar of white. Barnacle geese are much

Shelducks sweep their bills across mud to pick up tiny shellfish

more boldly patterned with black, white and blue-grey, with the face white or cream. Barnacles are special geese of some northern estuaries and islands, especially the Solway and Islay, and are rare in the south.

Barnacle geese are grazers on short grass

On the water a whole succession of interesting birds appears as the tide sweeps in. It is often best to sit and watch as the channels fill and the marshes flood. Cormorants move up with the rising water and there may be ducks such as goldeneyes, scaup and red-breasted mergansers, as well as great crested grebes and, in some places, black-necked or Slavonian grebes too.

It is always essential to remember, though, that estuaries and salt marshes are dangerous places: NEVER put yourself in a position in which you might be cut off or swept away by a rising tide.

THE MAGIC OF THE SALT MARSH

The salt marsh above the muddy beach is itself an important habitat. On the strand line in winter there will be rock pipits and, on the east coast, snow buntings or more rarely, shore larks. Greenfinches and starlings also take advantage of the flotsam and jetsam along the tideline.

Starlings are among several land birds to be found on marshes

Finches feed on the drier marshes, including one, the twite, which is almost entirely restricted to such places in winter. With it may be linnets and more greenfinches, even perhaps a few goldfinches. They attract predators and sparrowhawks which often zip across a marsh, while hen harriers are frequent hunters. Merlins hunt finches and small waders, short-eared owls prefer voles, while peregrines haunt many estuaries, ready to take a duck or a large wader in a lightning swoop.

Peregrines are birds of sea cliffs and inland crags and quarries all year round, but some move to the coast in winter and create havoc with the birds there. You can usually tell when one of these predators is about by the reaction of the other species. Starlings feed in large flocks on marshes and their sharp, urgent 'zic' calls tell of the appearance of a hawk or falcon.

Estuaries and low, sandy headlands in East Anglia are rich in shorebirds

Summer salt marsh

In summer, the salt marsh is a quite different place, much more benign, although you can still be caught by the tide.

Noise and busy activity fill the air around a black-headed gull colony

Black-headed gulls nest on many marshes, usually in a tangle of sea lavender, glasswort or sea asters. With them, or perhaps slightly removed on a higher, shingly or sandy ridge, there will be common terns. They are superb, slender, grey and white birds with jet black caps (unlike the black-headed gulls whose heads are really dark brown). Terns have an urgency and almost a hysteria when disturbed that will leave you in no doubt that you are intruding. Take note: they are sensitive to disturbance and, if you blunder into a colony by mistake, leave quickly to avoid serious losses of eggs and chicks.

Redshanks are always on the salt marsh (although they are found in many other habitats too) and are likely to reveal their presence by their sudden, loud, high-pitched calls. They are easily recognised by the broad band of white at the back of each wing and the white wedge on the lower back. If you see them feeding, they look duller, brown birds, but their red legs, medium-length bills and frequent bobbing of the head and body make them simple birds to identify.

Redshanks probe for small invertebrate food

COASTAL LAGOONS

Coastal lagoons are now mostly features of nature reserves, as those that have not been protected have generally been drained. They can be very good places indeed for the birdwatcher, all year round.

In winter they have a selection of wildfowl, like the nearby marshes, but with a better chance of seeing good views of shovelers, teal, wigeon and gadwalls. Black-headed, common, herring and other gulls are bound to be about, testing your abilities in their immature plumages but fairly obvious when adult.

Minsmere is a reserve managed for its shallow-water and island habitats

Black-tailed godwits feed in shallow water but nest in tussocky grass

Spring brings some migrant waders, sometimes in glorious breeding colours: the deep reds of black- and bar-tailed godwits, the paler brick red of knots, the lovely dunlins with inky-black belly patches, lapwings in glossy green and black with purple and bronze reflections. Greenshanks, green and common sandpipers and many more species are likely.

In summer some waders breed – redshanks, snipe, ringed plovers – and if you are in East Anglia or North Kent, you might strike lucky and see avocets. These elegant black and whiter-than-white waders, with their unique upcurved bills, nest in greater numbers than they have done for a century and in winter can be seen on a number of southern estuaries.

COASTAL GRAZING

The lagoons are mostly surrounded by a strip of mud and shingle, then rough grazing, perhaps with cattle or sheep. This hinterland is wild enough and full of sufficient food plants to attract a good variety of birds, especially during migration.

The shingle is good for ringed plovers while dry mud is favoured by little ringed plovers. Canada geese blunder about on the shore and, in most places, there will be a pair or two of feral greylag geese. Even a few unlikely-looking pheasants venture out from the vegetation to feed on the shingle ridges.

Where there are thistles and teasels, so there will be goldfinches and linnets. Sometimes, in fields of thistles and ragworts along the coastal strip, goldfinches reach substantial numbers, although rarely the hundreds that flock in Mediterranean countries. Stonechats like the tall stems of these bigger plants that give them a view across the grass, while wheatears and whinchats call in on migration, in spring and autumn.

In damper spots, especially where there are farm animals, yellow wagtails stay to nest. They are active and elegant, bringing a spot of vivid colour and vibrant activity to the meadows around the lagoons. In the autumn, if the lagoon is edged with taller growth, such as reeds or lank sedges, yellow wagtails, swallows and martins pour in each evening to spend the night clinging to stems above the water, safe from ground predators.

The avocet is a specialist wader of shallow, salty lagoons

ON THE BEACH

Sand and shingle beaches create difficult conditions for any form of life: they are mobile, and contain little microscopic or plant life in the spaces between the fine grains of sand or the larger, grinding, rolling pebbles of shingle. It is hard to get a toe hold here, and winds, high spring tides and frost all add to the problems of an environment that may, in any case, be subject to flooding by salt water and exposure to the air twice a day.

This is a typical sand and shingle beach bird: the ringed plover

Where the shingle ridges (or banks of shells) rise above the tideline into a semi-permanent form, they can be used by nesting birds. Here the ringed plover is at home, its black, white and brown pattern breaking up its outline in the strong light and shade of a pebble beach as it sits, motionless, on its eggs. It must move to sandier, or muddier, places to feed.

Oystercatchers also nest on shingle banks, using the cover of invading plants at the more stable edge of the beach if they can. Their eggs, however, are as well-camouflaged as the plover's and hard to spot.

Little terns are the other typical inhabitants of a shingle beach, nesting close to the tideline: so close, in fact, that their nests are often washed away in summer storms. Like all these beach-nesters, they are suffering from the increased disturbance from holiday-makers, dog-walkers, motorbikers, four-wheel drive vehicles, even helicopters landing in the middle of colonies. Only by direct wardening and fencing-off of colonies have they been helped to survive in southern Britain.

Little terns prefer shelving beaches of shingle or broken shells

Outside the breeding season the sandiest beaches hold rather few waders compared with mud, but sanderlings run the length of the beach along the tide's edge, picking up morsels disturbed by the waves. Gulls gather, of course, usually resting rather than feeding although some will use sandy beaches for opening shellfish, which they drop onto the firm wet sand from a great height.

Sand dunes are rather different, because, although they are mobile and exposed, they are much more stable in the short-term, usually with a covering of marram grass and, if they form large, permanent dunes, willow scrub and a variety of special duneland plants. Rabbits burrow into the sand and their

No other wader runs in and out with the waves quite so nimbly as the sanderling

abandoned holes make ideal nest sites for shelducks, especially if they have the added shelter of a bramble bush. Many shelducks nest far from the water, with a special feeding territory on the beach, to which they lead their newly-hatched ducklings.

Sandwich terns nest in dunes, in big, noisy, fluctuating colonies which may be there for a few years and gone the next. They are shy and highly-strung and the least disturbance is likely to ruin a whole season's breeding effort: with all terns, it is wisest to keep well away from their colonies while they are nesting.

Sandwich terns are large, aggressive terns but easily disturbed

MUDDY BEACHES

Muddy beaches are, in the main, richer than sandy ones, as the finer silts and muds make a more stable home for plants, algae, shellfish and marine worms, which in turn attract the birds. The environment, regularly swamped by salt water and exposed to drying winds and freshwater rainfall, is a peculiar mix which makes great demands on any form of life struggling to survive there.

A muddy estuary is said to be several times richer, or more productive, than the best farmland: certainly a decent bit of mud is likely to be home to millions of tiny snails and worms. These are the stuff of life for wading birds from all over the northern hemisphere: here, flightlines from Greenland, Iceland, Scandinavia and Siberia coincide and great flocks of knots,

dunlins, godwits and others pass the autumn, winter and spring months while their northern homes are dark and frozen.

Grey plovers defend small feeding territories in winter

You have to be at the right place with a rising tide to see the birds at their best, although, if you prefer close views of a few rather than the impact of the masses, you can often stalk individuals or groups of waders at low tide and get to know them better. Most beaches will have a few dunlins and curlews, ringed plovers and redshanks, but you may have to find a good estuary for a chance of knots, bar-tailed godwits and grey plovers. You will quickly learn which waders not to expect on an open beach: birds like snipe, green and wood sandpipers, common sandpipers, lapwings and golden plovers are wetland species, certainly, but prefer more shelter, so brackish lagoons, flooded fields, ditch systems and the like attract them, not the wide open beach.

◀ Mud at the sea's edge is extremely rich biologically

Knots rise in great flocks and twist and turn, now silver, now grey, looking like swarms of insects or clouds of smoke at long range. On the ground they tend to advance in denser groups than feeding dunlins and they look a bit bigger, greyer and more chunky. They are 'in between' birds, not so big as a redshank and not so small as a dunlin or ringed plover, nor are they very long-legged or long-billed. In spring and late summer you should find some in glorious summer plumage: in autumn, young birds have an exquisite pattern of lacy feather edgings above and a flush of salmon-pink beneath.

The ubiquitous dunlin

Dunlins, meanwhile, are smaller, with a bill that just slightly curves downwards. They have more marked wing bars and a black centred rump with bright white sides (on a knot the rump is just dull grey). They are lively, shuffling about like beach mice as they feed, often nervously flying a few yards then running back to the best feeding spot. In winter they are dull grey-brown above, white below, but beware the effects of light and shade in these exposed places. They can look warm brown to almost silvery grey, and on a dull day with reflections upwards from a wet beach, may even seem to be almost black on top and gleaming white beneath. Rarely will they look exactly as they do in a book, which has to paint an 'average' picture in flat, bright lighting.

In spring flocks of dunlins often make rippling, churring choruses as they begin to practise their summer songs: then they also have handsome summer plumage with rusty-coloured backs and a black square on the belly.

Dunlins nest in marshes and high, damp moorland, but spend the winter on the coast

Curlews are pale brown with dark streaks all over, but at a distance they have a habit of looking very dark. Out on the mud a resting curlew, or group of curlews, looks hunched and round-backed, big and lumpy compared with other waders. Indeed, with their heads tucked in, they look like long-legged young gulls. In flight they are gull-like, too, rather big, slow and long-winged for waders: but then, their heads are held forward and the long, downcurved bill is an instant giveaway. Only the whimbrel has a bill approaching this length and shape, but whimbrels are smaller, darker, quicker in flight and more stocky-looking, and the bill is a little more 'bent' than smoothly-curved.

The chief glory of the curlew is its song, which you may hear on a beach although it is best over some northern moor: it is a long, ecstatic, liquid bubbling sound, one of Europe's finest bird songs.

Bar-tailed godwits look curlew-like but straight-billed in a book: in reality, they are quite considerably smaller (although still a couple of sizes up from a redshank) and they have subtly different colours. Often they have a more buffy-peachy look about the chest than a curlew and tend to look paler at long range. Their bills are long (sometimes remarkably so) and have a distinct, slight upcurve to them.

Black-tailed godwits in winter are darker, greyer, plainer birds than bar-taileds (bar-taileds look streaked like curlews on top, black-taileds are not). They have straighter bills, sometimes equally long, and longer legs, which may be particularly evident

(especially when the bird is wading) 'above the knee' – the shinbone is markedly longer, giving a more upstanding look. Any doubt is quickly dispelled if the bird takes flight or flaps its wings. Whereas a bar-tailed is mottled with a white rump, the black-tailed is boldly contrasted, with dark wings marked by a long, central band of white and the white rump sharply contrasted against the jet-black tail.

Black-tailed godwits in breeding plumage

Black-tailed godwits winter on coastal mudflats, especially in the south and west

OUT TO SEA

OPEN ESTUARY

Out in the open estuary, the water is relatively sheltered compared with the open sea (although it can still work up a good chop) and the opportunity to see some wildfowl is often worth taking.

Again it is best as the tide rises, so that the birds come closer to a particularly favoured lookout, perhaps the headland or sand spit at the estuary mouth. Cormorants are common (shags are usually not, as they like rockier shores) and in winter, especially in the west, there may be great northern divers. They are hard to follow as they dive so often and may move 100 metres or more underwater, so it is difficult to spot them soon enough to get a good view before they dive under again.

Estuaries are exciting places for the birdwatcher

Many wildfowl are rare inland but numerous around our shores: scaup are commonest in the north

Small grebes on estuaries in autumn and winter may be Slavonian, black-necked, more rarely little, or occasionally even red-necked (while great cresteds are much more often on the sea than many people imagine). They, too, take some watching as they float like corks but dive with ease: care is needed to be really sure which one you are watching.

Ducks from more open seas may enter estuaries with a rising tide, giving welcome closer views: scaup are frequent in the north, long-tailed ducks more localised (but in some Scottish firths splendid, colourful, noisy flocks come in with the eiders), and scoters tend to be more often oiled, tired or in some other way unusual if they are in the estuary itself. Red-breasted mergansers haunt the estuaries of Scotland (often in good-sized flocks), and, in lesser numbers Wales and southern England: watch them in spring when parties of males display to females.

OPEN SEA

The open sea is a great place for birds but difficult for birdwatchers: generally speaking, most seabirds prefer to stay away from land unless they have to come to the nest.

The fulmar is related to petrels, shearwaters and albatrosses: a real ocean-going bird

The best way to see them, therefore, is to get a boat and go out to them (this is not so difficult: a cross-Channel ferry or a ferry across the Irish Sea can be excellent). Short of that, it is best to find a headland that sticks out into the sea and may intercept passing seabirds. There are plenty of good places: St. Ives in Cornwall, Portland Bill and Beachy Head on the Channel coasts, Flamborough, Filey Brigg, Hartlepool and Fife Ness on the North Sea and so on. Much depends on the weather: an onshore wind is usually best, but complex movements of seabirds are often best seen when a storm has displaced them and they then return to their normal routes after the winds have subsided.

Fulmars and gannets are not so hard to find and may be easy to see in many places, as they have long breeding seasons and stay near to cliffs for months. Storm and Leach's petrels are much more difficult, as they are small and hard to spot at long range and come to land only at night. They are best seen from ships or in a good gale on the west coast.

Manx shearwaters are similar (also coming to land at night) but rather easier to spot, being bigger and less apt to keep out of sight of land. Most good headlands have shearwaters passing from time to time and, in summer, the promontories of western Scotland and west Wales are usually good for watching flocks of shearwaters gathering ready to go ashore on their breeding islands after dark.

Gannets feed on large, muscular fish such as mackerel

Cliffs

Sea cliffs provide many of our seabirds with the solid base they need for breeding: literally a place to nest above the edge of the waves. The best are in the north and west but seabirds breed in isolated spots all around our coasts: magic places like Bempton Cliffs near Flamborough Head, Skomer Island in Dyfed, St. Abbs Head, Fowlsheugh (south of Aberdeen) and the Caithness cliffs give everyone a chance to enjoy seabirds in vast numbers. If you can get there, the cliffs of Orkney and Shetland are often in another league again.

The typical inhabitants of a sea cliff will usually be gulls (herring gulls especially), with kittiwakes in most larger colonies. The kittiwake is an ocean-going

Sheer cliffs near clean seas have marvellous concentrations of breeding seabirds

gull, calling its name to aid identification but unique in the way that groups nest together, their nests somehow stuck on to improbably small ledges and bumps on the sheer cliff wall. Some colonies number tens of thousands of pairs.

Equally adept at using tiny ledges on sheer cliffs (but laying eggs directly onto the rock, with no nest) are guillemots, also numbering tens of thousands at the best sites: like many small, brown and white penguins. Razorbills (black and white and even more penguin-like) are nearly always fewer, often tucked away into deep cavities and clefts. These two (which, together with the puffin, are auks) form great rafts of birds on the sea beneath the cliffs and, with the kittiwakes, create constant noise and activity in a seabird colony, which is one of the most intensely vibrant expressions of life in the world.

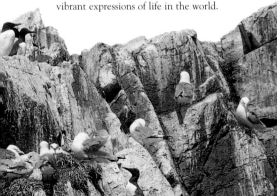

Puffins nest in burrows and under rocks, rather than on open ledges, so they are often seen in the fallen scree and rubble of a sloping cliff, in the deeper clefts of a sheer rock face, or, most particularly, on the grassier slopes above the cliff top. They are incurably nosy, always minding other puffins' business and getting into fights and scuffles. They are also quite confiding where humans are concerned, and invariably invite people to try to get that little bit closer: beware. Steep slopes above cliffs are extraordinarily dangerous places and great care must always be exercised. Best of all, go to a place like South stack on Anglesey or Bempton Cliffs in Humberside and look from specially-made viewpoints.

Cormorants nest on broad cliff ledges, often quite high, and shags nest on ledges and in caves, sometimes low down. Shags are smaller, greener, more shiny and snaky-looking than cormorants, in spring decorated with forward-curving tufts on their foreheads. In the water they look rounder-headed and slimmer-billed; in flight they are quicker and often hug the wave-tops, rarely flying so high as cormorants which are even capable of soaring about impressively above a colony.

The tallest promontories on the cliff edge will be taken over by great black-backed gulls. These are less densely colonial than other gulls, more territorial, and their greater bulk and span and blacker upperparts give them an air of distinction and power. They are, indeed, dominant among gulls in any gathering.

Herring gulls like broken cliffs and rock slabs. They are easy to tell, with their silvery-grey backs, black and white wingtips and yellow bills with red near the tip. Lesser black-backed gulls are slimmer, longer-looking than herring gulls, with vivid yellow (not pink) legs and dark, slaty-grey backs: they tend to prefer flatter island-tops and hummocky ground with heather, thrift or sea campion.

Most people know the puffin, although they have to travel north to see them

ISLANDS

Islands offshore, often under the rocky cliffs, provide more secluded places for terns to nest. Terns are often vulnerable to disturbance and predation (by foxes, hedgehogs, rats and cats) and an island gives extra security. These long-winged, long-tailed, short-legged birds simply are not made for sheer cliffs and need flatter ground.

Arctic terns nest on rocky islands and reefs all around the northern and western coasts of Britain and Ireland. They are commoner than common terns in the north but the reverse is true on the softer coasts of

the south and east and in many western Scottish sea lochs. Both are red-legged, red-billed birds with silvery upperparts and jet black caps: subtle details of wing pattern, bill colour, leg length and so on separate them but they are not easy to distinguish. You know if you are too close to their nests, because they dive and scream at you: arctics, in particular (on the Farne Islands for example) are liable to draw blood from the scalps of people who venture into the colony. Because of the disturbance (which may let a crafty crow or gull nip in to steal a chick) it is best to keep away.

Arctic terns breed as far north as the Arctic and winter close to the Antarctic

Roseate terns are sadly rare and have suffered years of decline. Numbers are now stable, at a low level, but many old colonies have gone. They like to nest in little hollows and under tree mallow plants: even in nest boxes!

◀ Islands offshore have some species that would be vulnerable to disturbance and predators on the mainland

NORTHERN ISLES

The northern isles around the far northern tip of Scotland and, especially, in the Orkney and Shetland archipelagos, have some special birds. Great and arctic skuas are bold, aggressive, gull-like birds that will attack anything and everything that comes near a nest, including you. Great skuas may whack you over the head but it is their intimidating low-level attack at great speed that is most disconcerting: they are, after all, the size of a large gull and much more heavily built. Arctic skuas might resort, instead, to playing the 'broken-wing trick', pretending they are injured in an effort to lure you away.

Both of these wonderful birds are predatory and take a lot of food by robbing gulls, terns and puffins in

a short, breathless aerial chase. An arctic skua (better still, a pair) chasing a kittiwake over the sea is wonderful to watch: the silver bird doing its utmost to escape the dark brown one, which matches every twist and turn in a strenuous aerobatic performance until the gull coughs up a fish.

These northern islands are bleak places, but oddly enough are homes to wrens: often special wrens, too. Some island groups have populations of wrens that have become so isolated, for so long, that they have diverged from mainland wrens in their colour and the amount of dark barring on their feathers – so, look out for Shetland, Fair Isle or St. Kilda wrens if ever you have the chance.

Arctic skuas specialise in stealing fish from other birds

◀ Shetland and Orkney have some of the bleakest landscapes in Britain, and some of the rarest birds

SWAMPS

Some of the low-lying coasts, especially in East Anglia, are backed by flooded ground that has developed into reed swamps. These reed beds – extensive stands of common reed growing up from shallow water – are rare and fragile habitats which are home to some exciting birds. Sadly, they naturally dry out as the reed litter builds up and willows take over. This is a natural cycle, but nowadays it is unlikely that the natural sequence of events includes the flooding of more land for new reed beds to develop to replace those that are lost, so, if we want reed bed birds, we must manage the beds to keep them wet.

The dense stems of tall reeds create a demanding habitat for birds

This is the only hope for the bittern, a secretive, streaky-brown heron that likes its reeds especially wet, so it can catch eels without having to venture into the open. There are fewer than 20 pairs left in Britain: you may hear one in summer, giving a deep, resonant 'boom' like a giant breath of air across the mouth of some hidden bottle.

Bearded tits love reeds, too, and breed nowhere else. They are not really titmice at all, but are long-tailed, lively, remarkably pretty little birds best found by following up their sharp, ringing (or 'kissing') pinging calls. Then you might see one or two dart across the reed tops, trailing a long tail, like a tiny, tawny pheasant. In calm, warm weather you should be lucky enough to see them feeding near the reed tops, and see the male's lovely blue head with black moustache and orange-yellow bill. You need to be in Norfolk, Suffolk, Humberside or at Leighton Moss in Lancashire to stand a real chance of seeing one.

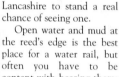

Open water and mud at the reed's edge is the best place for a water rail, but often you have to be content with hearing them: they squeal and grunt like piglets. Frosty weather often brings them out into the open from the seclusion of their favoured reed bed lairs.

Bitterns have become exceedingly rare as reedbeds have dried out in recent years

Reed beds with associated freshwater are always great places for birds and special reserves, such as those in Suffolk, along the north Norfolk coast and the Norfolk Broads, are well worth a visit.

In summer reed buntings (males with black heads and white collars, and a short, tuneless, jingling song) join the reed warblers and sedge warblers in the dawn chorus. They are all a lot less vocal by day. In the evenings, barn owls often hunt around such places.

In winter, the hunters are more varied, with short-eared owls by day as well as dusk and hen harriers

Marsh harriers are able to spread into small patches of reeds so long as they are not persecuted

Grey herons need shallow water and a good supply of small fish

also often abroad in the twilight. Marsh harriers breed in small numbers in reed beds but are less likely in winter as most move south. The hen harrier is easy to distinguish, being paler grey with black wingtips (males) or brown, streaky underneath, with a crisp white rump (females and young) whereas the marsh harrier is a mix of grey, brown, rufous and black (males) or dark chocolate brown with yellow-cream on the head.

As well as the expected waterside birds – grey herons, Canada geese, mallards and moorhens, for example – reed beds attract a variety of others that may be unexpected but are equally part of the birdlife there. Blue tits forage in reeds very often, easily dealing with the vertical stems of this peculiar, enclosed habitat as they tear into the seed heads and rip away leaves in search of insects and spiders. More of a shock may be the sight of a big, pale brown, long-tailed bird dashing into the reeds or flying out of sight before you get a good look at it: it is only a female pheasant, a frequent reed bed species!

MIGRATION

One of the special things about birds, something that has puzzled people for thousands of years, is the large scale migration of huge numbers every spring and autumn. The exodus of literally hundreds of millions of warblers, swallows, martins and others from Europe, heading into Africa every year, reminds us that birds are international and to protect them we must have a truly global perspective. We have all too often found birds declining in Britain because of something happening to them elsewhere: white-throats, for example, used to be abundant but crashed to a quarter of their past level after droughts in the Sahel.

Likewise, we are host to millions of waders and wildfowl every winter and, should we in Britain abuse our estuaries and wetlands, the birds and people of great swathes of the northern hemisphere would suffer.

Birds migrate because they are able to take advantage of opportunities in one part of the world which last only for part of the year. Many species breed far to the north: in summer, there is an abundance of insects and their larvae and, it must also be remembered, 24 hours of daylight in which to eat them and feed them to growing chicks. This is a super abundance of food and the chance to exploit it that millions of birds take advantage of.

In autumn, however, they have to move south because these northern areas are becoming cold, dark and lifeless.

Such movements of birds on the grand scale provide us with every opportunity to see a greater variety, in greater numbers, with an ever-changing list of birds to watch all through the year.

Birds which breed around the Arctic and Northern Europe and spend the winter in Africa migrate along the western seaboard of Europe and Africa, or concentrate on the shortest sea-crossings over the Mediterranean

THE URGENCY OF SPRING

The spring rush is a hectic, urgent affair. Birds are moving north and they must get there before the territories they seek are taken up by others. Males are often moving before females, to stake out their claims: as soon as they are on site in spring they begin to sing and dispute territory.

If we see a migrant pausing on its way north, it is likely to be gone next day: they have no time to spare to hang around. There are, though, plenty of birds that have to linger until late spring, even early summer. The knots, turnstones, grey plovers and bar-tailed godwits that must breed in the high Arctic cannot go too soon. The Arctic will not be ready for them until late May and they cannot risk arriving to find deep snow and no food. So our estuaries are full of birds until much later than might be expected – our

'winter visitors' might be with us until May and back again by August.

Woodlands are quickly filled with new arrivals. A local patch such as a gravel pit with mixed marshy areas and patches of woodland or thickets is ideal for watching migration in action. March will see the first chiffchaffs and sand martins, perhaps little ringed plovers. April sees a movement of birds that may have been in Britain all winter but still migrate to different places to breed – meadow pipits, reed buntings, pied wagtails. Then, day by day, we see the first swallows, cuckoos, sedge warblers, willow warblers and blackcaps, reed warblers and yellow wagtails. It is an annual delight to enjoy the return of old friends: many of them the self same birds, returning to the very same tree to sing again as before.

One of the most welcome signs of spring is the delicate song of the willow warbler

CHANGING SCENE

Spring often brings warm southerly winds, and birds that have travelled north from Africa to find a breeding site in southern Europe may be swept far beyond the normal range and end up here for us to enjoy. They are strays, but will in all probability get back south to where they belong with little trouble.

Little egrets suddenly became frequent on the estuaries of southern England in the early 1990s

These rarities are of little importance in the ornithological scheme of things, but the added spice and excitement they provide, after a long winter, is all to the good.

The occasional woodchat shrike, hoopoe, night heron, purple heron, black kite or red-footed falcon may come our way.

Some of these birds have a greater significance than we might first believe. Black kites have long been predicted as new breeding birds in Britain, and numbers have increased, but they have not yet settled. The same was once said of serins: but the serin did actually go so far as to nest in England on a few occasions. Now, however, it seems to have withdrawn again. Cetti's warblers did the same in the 1970s and have become established, regular breeders now, but still decline severely in a hard winter.

What next? The big rush of the 1990s has been of little egrets. Not long ago one of these small, pure-white herons with black legs and yellow feet would have raised the birdwatching temperature anywhere, bringing in the crowds. It still does in the midlands and north, but along the south coast there are now scores of them, witness to a sudden, unpredictable (and unpredicted) swing in fortunes and extension of range.

Hoopoes are recorded every year in Britain but just where and when is unpredictable

AUTUMN AT LEISURE

Autumn migration is altogether more relaxed than spring. After all, there is no need to get in first to find the best breeding territory and attract a mate, although we do know that many species will have winter territories and finding and defending a good one can be vital to survival. The flocks of feeding waders on an estuary, for example, may look like random scatterings, but in truth there is a great deal of competition going on and it is a matter of life and death. The grey plover on the best bit of beach is going to survive, while the weaker, subordinate bird pushed out to the inferior edge might well succumb before the winter is out.

Many wading birds migrate through the UK in autumn: the green sandpiper does not breed and is scarce in winter, but relatively numerous in autumn

Autumn sees greater numbers of birds than spring, of course, by virtue of the fact that the year's crop of young will have increased the stock, temporarily. Most of these will die and migration is a severe test for them, but meanwhile we see migrating flocks of birds such as swallows and martins and groups of exciting waders, like little stints and curlew sandpipers, that may be very largely juvenile birds of the year.

Because migrations begin immediately once breeding is over, 'autumn' migration may actually start in June (with flocks of lapwings and long-distance travellers such as green sandpipers), but with the somewhat leisurely approach taken by many small birds, as well as the gradual movements of wildfowl, it may continue until December.

Swallows gather on wires: a sign of impending departure for Africa

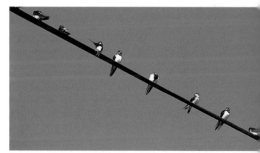

Migration is often undertaken in flocks and we can see the gatherings of certain species grow day by day. Easiest, perhaps, are the flocks of swallows and martins that build up on telephone wires (or which sunbathe on tiled roofs). In the evenings these flocks may find special places to roost together and then we have a real spectacle to enjoy. Reed beds often attract hundreds of pied and yellow wagtails, together with thousands of swallows and martins and perhaps tens of thousands of starlings. As dusk falls and the birds arrive, so the sparrowhawks and hobbies become alert, too, ready to take advantage of this bumper crop of edible bird life.

Rarely do we see other small birds in big numbers, however: most warblers, chats, flycatchers, nightingales and so on move at night, silent and invisible to our eyes. If, however, a fine, clear night in northwestern Europe stimulates the birds to fly up and away, and they then meet strong winds and cloudy skies out over the North Sea, we might benefit from their ill-luck. In such conditions, especially if the coast looms through mist or drizzly rain, we may see a 'fall' of migrants, all of which have drifted too far west and, tired and hungry, are ready to drop to the first bit of land they encounter.

In some years coastal localities in the north and east may find birds by the thousand, literally crawling everywhere: goldcrests, pied flycatchers, redstarts, wheatears, whinchats and others fill every bush. With them, will be a few rarer birds, such as barred warblers, wrynecks and red-backed shrikes. All is excitement and anticipation for the lucky birdwatcher who happens to be in the right place, at the right time.

Other species are much more discreet. Wood warblers, for example, are common enough in western and southern oak and beech woods, but they seem to fly from the breeding site right away to Africa, and return the same way. One day they are there: one day they are not. And they are almost never seen on the coast, away from their breeding woods.

Whinchats breed in the north and west but may be seen along the east coast on migration

AUTUMN WADERS

Waders are much in evidence in autumn: even the smallest inland pool might attract a common sandpiper or a ruff.

Early on the adults appear: July and August sees sandpipers and shanks, godwits and plovers, often in the worn remnants of their stunning summer plumages. In August we might see a handful of curlew sandpipers, still blotchy red, or spotted redshanks in coal-black feathers. Then they go and the next wave, in September or even early October, will be of similar species but often in greater numbers, and these are the juveniles. Now we have little stints in 'classic' rusty, black and cream-striped juvenile plumage, curlew sandpipers patterned in grey and buff, with immaculate peachy breasts, spotted redshanks in barred brown and grey: a whole new set of plumages to learn, sort out and enjoy.

Watch the juveniles

Not many years ago, field guides had 'summer plumage' and 'winter plumage' waders: the winter birds were a mixture of real winter plumages and autumn juveniles, but for most species autumn juveniles were ignored, so that the majority of birds that the ordinary birdwatcher would see in Britain were not covered at all! No wonder things were confusing. Now, with much more interest in the detail of particular plumages, in ageing and sexing birds in the field, it is far clearer what is going on and the books have generally caught up. Unfortunately some authors still prefer to generalise, and autumn juveniles are, therefore, still omitted and people are left in a state of disappointed and confused (rather than blissful) ignorance.

This juvenile curlew sandpiper is a few weeks old and will have been reared on Arctic tundra: it will spend a week or two in England on its way south

Juvenile little stints are sometimes extremely tame when they appear in Britain in August and September

WILD GEESE

Later in autumn wild geese arrive from Iceland and northern Europe or Siberia. They are very special birds: for some, the essence of winter and wildness, the sign of the changing seasons.

Wild geese are exciting winter birds: these are white-fronted geese

Brent geese are, in some ways, the least romantic, being relatively confiding (after years of protection with no shooting, which shows what an effect that activity has on the rest) and living in the estuaries of the south and east. In recent years they have taken to feeding on agricultural land, too, much to the chagrin of many farmers. Nevertheless, they are truly wild geese and they have travelled from the far north of Siberia to be with us.

Barnacle geese come from Spitsbergen to the Solway Firth and from Greenland to northern and western isles, especially Islay. They are spectacular, handsome geese, immaculate in grey, black and white, and form large, irregular, yapping packs. Compared with the average flock of semi-tame, semi-resident Canada geese, they are altogether more exciting.

It is the grey geese that capture the imagination most. Bean geese are very rare and largely restricted to Norfolk in winter. Greylag geese are somewhat devalued, in a way, because many now live all year round in places where they have been introduced. They still arrive in numbers, however, from Iceland. Perhaps the white-fronted geese (now sadly reduced in most areas, and best seen at Slimbridge in Gloucestershire) and pink-footed geese (most common in Norfolk, Lancashire and much of lowland Scotland) are the wildest and most romantic spirits, genuinely wary, elusive and unapproachable in most places. They form the classic goose flocks in Vs and chevrons and fly over at dusk with evocative and beautiful calls. Somehow, a wild goose chase, if it succeeds in giving good views of a good flock of birds, has an incomparable satisfaction about it. You need local knowledge, patience, warm and waterproof clothing, a good telescope and some luck, but to see wild geese well is a splendid experience.

RARITIES

EXCITING RARITIES

Autumn is also a good time for rarities. Migrants are on the move everywhere and it is possible to see almost anything, almost anywhere. The best thing about rarities is that they might turn up in front of anyone: they are not the exclusive preserve of experts. Of course, it may help to have some expertise to identify some of them, but there are rarities that are blindingly obvious (a white stork, for example, is not hard to work out!)

It helps to know something about the conditions that bring rarities to our shores and to have an idea of where best to look for them. It may take 20 years to find a rarity at an inland site, while the east coast in October is much more likely to be productive. There are special places, such as Fair Isle, the north Norfolk coast and the Isles of Scilly, where rarities are almost the norm.

Finding a rarity is the most exciting part: seeing one which someone else found and reported is great, but lacks the edge of discovery and surprise. There is no substitute for hard work and hours in the field if one wishes to find something good: but, by their very nature, rarities are unpredictable.

Now it is possible for anyone to see an extreme rarity within hours of its arrival, simply by dialling a rare bird line recorded message and following the latest instructions. Whereas some years ago a small band of enthusiasts had its own 'grapevine' and rare birds were greeted with small groups of excited people, a rarity now may be seen by literally thousands, some of whom may never even have heard of the bird before. Does it devalue the experience? It is for you to decide: birdwatching is a hobby and there are, mercifully, no rules, so no one can criticise others, however they decide to play the game.

Crowds of birdwatchers gathered where a rarity has been discovered still make the newspapers, but this is now a frequent sight

KEEPING THE RECORD STRAIGHT

If rarity-spotting is a game, then it may as well be played by the rules. If there is a scientific value, then, again, the record should most certainly be kept straight.

With this in mind, a whole network of county bird recorders has long been established to gather records and publish them in annual bird reports – not just of rarities, but of all species, so that even the common ones can be monitored. For rarities, a common standard of assessment is achieved by the work of a national rarities committee in each European country. These work closely together to help build up a pattern of the changing status of rare birds.

In Britain, county bird reports will not publish rare bird records until they have the official stamp of approval from the British Birds Rarities Committee, an elected panel of experts that examines upwards of 1,000 reports annually. The committee itself publishes its own annual rare birds report.

If you see a rarity, you do not have to tell others, although you may like to remember that others will get enjoyment from sharing your good fortune, if circumstances allow. Whether or not you spread the news at the time, though, you would certainly be advised to send a report of the bird later, in writing, to the Committee so that the event can be put on permanent record and included in the national statistics. The address can be obtained from *British Birds*, Park Lane, Blunham, Bedford MK44 3NJ.

ONE STEP FURTHER

Handbooks

Handbooks are different from field guides. Field guides are exactly that – guides. They can help to a certain extent, but they are small, with space for a small amount of text and few pictures. They cannot provide all the information you would like.

Bigger handbooks are much more comprehensive: they are also much bigger, not meant to be taken out, and much more expensive. You may find that you would like a bigger, more complete book once you learn more about birds. The handbook of all the birds in Europe and North Africa – *The Birds of the Western Palearctic*, or BWP for short – is a real 'bible', but you will probably find a quick look at it in the local library is enough for you for a start.

Handbooks like this are to be referred to when you see something new: a bird behaving in a different way, or a different plumage, or a bird eating some odd sort of food. The handbook will tell you whether you have really seen something unusual, or that it is perfectly normal, but just something you haven't noticed before. Handbooks are essential references, but not everyday identification guides: so they come later.

Censusing

Once you begin to identify birds you might like to go further into the world of birdwatching. Perhaps counting the birds and mapping them is one line of exploration that will appeal.

There are many ways of counting and censusing birds. Simple things are counting wildfowl on the local lake or reservoir, or counting the numbers of gulls at a roost. This may seem obvious, but you can do a lot of useful work like this. Over the years the counts build up into a useful set of data to show population changes. If you count ducks, you can note the numbers of males and females; with gulls, you can watch how the proportions of different species and the percentage of each age group changes with time. Often you may have the same total month after month, but it is made up of quite different proportions of males and females, adults and immatures, in each count. The patterns reveal a lot about the lifestyles, migrations and local movements of birds.

Common gulls in summer plumage: winter and immature ones look quite different

For example, common gulls on the south coast may be all adults in winter. In early spring half may be adults, half immatures. By late spring, the adults have all gone north to their breeding grounds, but much bigger numbers of immatures have arrived from farther south. On the local lake, at the same time, you may have had 20 goldeneyes all winter: 15 females and immatures, 5 adult males. By late spring, you could have 25 – but now 20 males and only 5 females.

Census work is fascinating, especially if you keep at it over many years. Essentially, you count the number of breeding birds in a specified area each spring and summer. You may need to make nine or ten visits, perhaps a couple of hours each time, early in the morning. Use a large scale map and mark down all the birds you see: use special codes for singing birds, fighting

males, females building nests, adults feeding young and so on. Gradually you will build up a picture of what is there and where their territories lie.

A juvenile common gull: easily separated from its whiter parents

In this way you can see how numbers of warblers fluctuate from one summer to the next. You can watch wrens and goldcrests build up to high numbers in good years, only to crash again after a bad winter, before increasing once more. Other changes might be quite inexplicable; but some will be obvious, if the habitat changes. If a farmer changes a damp meadow to a cereal field, there will be no problems deciding why all the lapwings and snipe have disappeared.

For full details of census work and how to do it properly, write to The British Trust for Ornithology at The Nunnery, Thetford, Norfolk.

If you cannot gain access to a large area to census in full, you might at least be able to sample one, by doing a regular walk along a fixed route: perhaps a nature trail or a public footpath through farmland and woods. Carry out a simple transect, counting all the birds you see and hear on the way and marking them on a map.

Special counts run by the BTO and the Wildfowl & Wetlands Trust (based at Slimbridge, Gloucestershire) keep a national record of numbers of several kinds of birds. There are regular heronry counts (BTO) and periodic surveys of birds such as nightjars and corn buntings. The WWT runs a monthly count every winter, attempting to keep track of numbers of ducks, geese and swans nationwide. You can become the counter for a local lake, if you would like to join in.

The BTO and WWT between them also organise counts of all the waders and wildfowl on our estuaries, with coordinated high-tide counts all around our coasts. These have provided invaluable conservation information and are just some of the ways that ordinary, amateur birdwatchers do their bit for researching and protecting wild birds.

CLUBS AND SOCIETIES

There are many clubs to join and magazines to subscribe to for British birdwatchers. It is, really, too much to join or buy them all: it would cost a fortune. Instead, select the right ones for your level of interest, knowledge and aspirations.

The RSPB is one body that all birdwatchers should join as it fights to protect wild birds and their habitats nationwide, and internationally. It produces a glossy, informative, entertaining magazine, *Birds*, four times each year. The address is the RSPB, The Lodge, Sandy, Bedfordshire SG19 2DL.

The 'journal of record' in the UK is *British Birds*, a monthly journal or serious birdwatchers' magazine, with recent news, reports, rarities reports, identification papers, notes and letters and major scientific papers in a well-tried and tested mix of material: the address is given on page 224.

Commercial magazines on bookstalls currently include *Bird Watching*, a popular, glossy, up-to-date magazine with loads of news and photographs: the tabloid end, if you like. *Birdwatch* is a little more advanced, more expert, more controversial at times and worth a look. It is also available on the bookstalls as well as by subscription.

Locally, you really ought to join a county bird club and take advantage of its publications and programme of activities. The local county bird report is, especially, a fund of information on what you might see, when and where. You can then contribute your own reports to fill out the picture and make your hobby more constructive. *The Birdwatcher's Yearbook*, published by Buckingham Press, contains all the addresses you will ever need: buy it or peruse a copy at the library and you can decide just what to join and what to buy.

BIRDWATCHERS' CODE OF CONDUCT

1. The welfare of the birds must come first.
2. Its habitat is vital to a bird and therefore we must ensure that our activities do not cause damage.
3. Keep disturbance to a minimum at all times.
4. If you discover a rare bird breeding and feel that protection is necessary, inform the appropriate RSPB regional office. Otherwise it is best in almost all circumstances to keep the record strictly secret in order to avoid disturbance by other birdwatchers and attacks by egg-collectors.
5. Rare migrants or vagrants should not be harassed. If you discover one, consider the circumstances carefully before telling anyone.
6. The bird protection laws, as now embodied in the Wildlife and Countryside Act 1981, are the result of hard campaigning by previous generations of birdwatchers. As birdwatchers we must abide by them at all times and not allow them to fall into disrepute.
7. Respect the rights of landowners. Do not enter private land without permission.
8. Respect the rights of other people who also use the countryside. Do not interfere with their activities.
9. Much of our knowledge about birds is the result of meticulous record-keeping by our predecessors. Make sure you help to add to tomorrow's knowledge by sending records to your county bird recorder.
10. When birdwatching abroad, behave as you would at home and adhere firmly to this code.

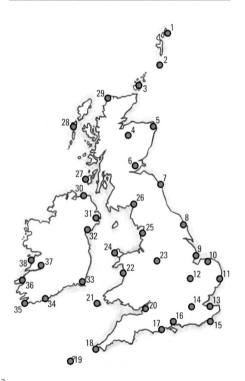

1. Shetland: whole complex of islands exciting for seabirds and migrants: RSPB reserve on Fetlar, seabird colonies at Hermaness, Noss

2. Fair Isle: marvellous small island with exciting seabirds and renowned selection of migrants in spring, summer and autumn

3. Orkney: rare breeding birds on many islands, excellent seabird cliffs and rare autumn migrants: RSPB reserves on North Hoy, Marwick Head

4. Loch Garten/Strath Spey: ancient forests have unique Scottish crossbill; also famous ospreys, crested tits. Nearby Cairngorms have dotterels and ptarmigan

5. Loch of Strathbeg: extraordinary area for large flocks of greylag and pink-footed geese, especially in autumn; also passing seabirds off Rattray Head, migrants

6. Loch Leven: RSPB visitor centre at Vane Farm – many thousands of wild geese in autumn

7. Farne Islands and Holy Island: islands have seabird colonies in summer, famed for their approachability in picturesque setting, including puffins, terns; in winter, Lindisfarne is a major wildfowl refuge

8. Bempton Cliffs and Flamborough Head: mainland gannet colony north of Bempton; also huge seabird colonies including a few puffins; famous migration watchpoint in spring and autumn with many rarities

9. Gibraltar Point: bird observatory in area of dunes and scrub: good all year

10. North Norfolk coast: string of marvellous reserves along the coast, encompassing sand and mudflats, low-lying wet pastures, reedbeds, lagoons, shingle beaches. Brilliant all year: breeding avocets, bearded tits, marsh harriers, terns; in

winter geese, scoters, eiders, harriers; in spring and autumn anything can turn up

11. East Suffolk: complex of broads and low-lying reedbeds with lagoons, woods, heath – RSPB reserve at Minsmere – bitterns, marsh harriers, bearded tits; in winter, divers, birds of prey

12. Rutland Water, Leicestershire & Rutland: reserve at western end (Egleton) and large numbers of wildfowl

13. North Kent: marshes and estuaries (Medway, Swale) full of birds; woodlands inland (e.g. Blean, Canterbury) exciting for typical woodland birds

14. London reservoirs: permits needed for most, but fine wildfowl sites and likely migrant watchpoints close to London

15. Dungeness: bird observatory and RSPB reserve – breeding gulls, terns, ducks, waders; migrants in spring and autumn

16. New Forest: explore whole area for woodland and heath birds, including woodlark, Dartford warbler

17. Poole Harbour and nearby Dorset heaths: wildfowl and waders, breeding nightjars, hobbies, Dartford warblers, chats

18. Land's End: whole area good for watching seabirds, especially passing by headlands in autumn; also autumn rarities

19. Isles of Scilly: seabirds (including petrels and shearwaters) breed; various rare migrants (e.g. herons and egrets, hoopoes, bee-eaters) in spring and a galaxy of rarities each autumn from North America, Europe and Siberia (often all at once)

20. Severn Estuary: includes Wildfowl & Wetlands Trust reserve and headquarters at Slimbridge – wildfowl, birds of

prey in winter

21. Pembrokeshire Islands, Dyfed: Skomer, Skokholm and Ramsey Islands each have seabird colonies, choughs, peregrines

22. Ynys-hir: RSPB reserve on the Dovey; nearby Mawddach reserve – west Wales estuaries with wildfowl and adjacent hills and woods with red kites, buzzards, wood warblers, pied flycatchers, dippers on streams

23. West Midland reservoirs: Blithfield and Belvide (Staffordshire) and Kingsbury Water Park (Warwickshire) have large wildfowl flocks autumn-spring, passage waders

24. South Stack: Anglesey has several good lakes and coastal reserves (e.g. Cemlyn Bay) with breeding gulls, terns, wildfowl; South Stack (RSPB) has seabird colonies, including puffins

25. Leighton Moss and Morecambe Bay: the Moss is a reedbed reserve with breeding bitterns, marsh harriers; the Bay is full of migrant waders at almost any time of year, with vast spring concentrations of knots

26. Solway: whole of Solway Firth area, especially north side, superb autumn-spring with large wildfowl flocks (including Greenland white-fronted, pink-footed, greylag and barnacle geese, wigeon, scoters, whooper swans). RSPB reserves at Loch Ken and Mersehead

27. Islay: one of the best of the Inner Hebrides, all year round, with many thousands of wildfowl including barnacle geese from autumn to late spring; also breeding choughs, harriers, eagles, corncrakes

28. Western Isles: the Uists are best for the visiting bird-watcher – RSPB reserve at Balranald; exciting seabird passage in spring; breeding corncrakes still maintain a toe-hold

29. Handa Island: Scottish Wildlife Trust reserve off Sutherland coast, full of breeding seabirds in dramatic setting; adjacent mainland has divers, eagles, ptarmigan

30. Rathlin Island: one of Ireland's best seabird colonies – RSPB reserve

31. Strangford Lough: a wonderful estuary with good views of brent geese, other wildfowl and waders from surrounding roads

32. Carlingford Lough: fine estuary for shorebirds, especially godwits and brent geese

33. Wexford Slobs: brilliant winter wildfowl refuge with many Greenland white-fronted geese

34. Southern Co. Cork estuaries: a succession of small estuaries west from Cork Harbour, all superb for close-up views of waders and wildfowl (especially black-tailed godwits), terns and possible rarities in autumn

35. Mizen Head: a remarkable place for watching seabirds (Manx and sooty shearwaters, storm petrels, gannets) passing offshore in autumn – local headlands, gardens and lagoons attract autumn rarities

36. Tralee Bay: winter wildfowl include brent geese, wigeon, teal, but the whole area is worth a look at any time; remember choughs on headlands close by

37. Shannon estuary complex: explore this wild wetland area at any season – migrant and breeding waders and excellent numbers of wildfowl in winter

38. Cliffs of Moher: precipitous seabird cliffs with fulmars, kittiwakes, guillemots, puffins

INDEX